A Royal Passion

A Royal Passion is the first book specifically devoted to the Sun King as a patron of architecture. Surveying such monuments as the Louvre, Versailles, the Invalides, Marly, and other buildings commissioned by Louis XIV, Robert Berger demonstrates why these buildings, gardens, urban spaces, and their decorations were so important to that monarch, serving as functional necessities, objects of aesthetic delight, and as political statements. The Sun King's patronage is viewed within the traditions of the "builder-prince," and his architecture is placed within the context of the political absolutism of his age.

A Royal Passion

Louis XIV as Patron of Architecture

Robert W. Berger

CAMBRIDGE
UNIVERSITY PRESS

Published by the Press Syndicate of the University of Cambridge
The Pitt Building, Trumpington Street, Cambridge CB2 1RP
40 West 20th Street, New York, NY 10011-4211, USA
10 Stamford Road, Oakleigh, Melbourne 3166, Australia

First published 1994

Printed in the United States of America

Library of Congress Cataloging-in-Publication Data
Berger, Robert W.
    A royal passion : Louis XIV as patron of architecture / Robert W.
Berger.
        p.   cm.
    Includes bibliographical references and index.
    ISBN 0-521-44029-7
    1. Classicism in architecture—France.   2. Architecture, Baroque—
France.   3. Architecture—France.   4. Architects and patrons—
France—History—17th century.   5. Louis XIV, King of France,
1638–1715—Contributions in architecture.   I. Title.
NA1046.B47   1994
724'.10'0944—dc20   92-17172
                                                                  CIP

A catalog record for this book is available from the British Library

ISBN 0-521-44029-7 hardback

To my wife, Susan Robbins Berger,
for all the years, in gratitude.

CONTENTS

Contents

ILLUSTRATIONS

PREFACE
AND ACKNOWLEDGMENTS

This book is at once a survey of the royal architecture of Louis XIV and a study of that monarch as patron. The Sun King has seemed for the most part remote and austere to his contemporaries and posterity, but I hope this book succeeds in revealing a more human dimension to the man through his enthusiasm for the building arts.

I would like to thank Martha Mel Edmunds for her critical reading of my pages on the Chapel of Versailles; Rochelle Ziskin for her critical reading of Chapter 12; Philippe Dugimont for help in translating a passage by Vauban and in arranging access to the Citadel of Lille; Sergent Michel Christophe of the 43ième Régiment d'Infanterie for escorting me around the Citadel and explaining its history and features in detail; Thomas Hedin and Betsy Rosasco for loans of photographs; and Michel Barbier for providing a pleasant excursion to Maintenon and Marly.

I would also like to thank my editor, Dr. Beatrice Rehl of Cambridge University Press, for her guidance and support of this project from its early stages.

Figure 1. Anonymous French Painter, *Louis XIV with the Plan of Saint-Cyr*, ca. 1687.
Musée National du Château de Versailles. (Photo: Réunion des Musées Nationaux.)

INTRODUCTION

This book is about a king who loved to build. We see him in a painting (Fig. 1), seated and wearing his coronation robes. He gazes out at the spectator while pointing to an architectural plan partly unrolled on the table beside him. The building can be identified: it is Saint-Cyr, a school for girls from noble but impecunious families. Its buildings were constructed in 1686–7 with royal funds, and to stress this point, the royal crown appears on the table, just above the furled part of the scroll. This portrait of Louis XIV, by an anonymous French artist, is contemporary with the erection of the school. The King was then forty-eight or forty-nine years old, already past the midpoint of a very long reign that lasted from 1643 to 1715.

The association of architecture and kingship reaches back to the early civilizations of the Middle East; we readily think of Mesopotamian kings and their ziggurats, Egyptian pharaohs and their pyramids, Solomon and his temple. There is a very long line of ruler – builders stretching from those early times to the era of Louis XIV. Even the type of portrait that shows the monarch with a drawing or model of a building he has sponsored has a long prehistory, going back to the medieval period (Fig. 2). What is distinctive about Louis XIV in this broad context is the extent of his architectural patronage, his close attention to details of design and construction, his active role, on at least one occasion, as a designer, and his instinctive understanding of the importance of architecture to statecraft. The Sun King is best remembered in architectural history for Versailles, the most famous palace and garden in the world. Less well-appreciated are the high aesthetic quality and innovative nature of many of his other buildings. This book parades Louis' commissions in generally chronological order so that the reader can grasp the development of his architecture through time. The book also attempts to make these creations more understandable and to

Figure 2. Byzantine Mosaic, *King William II of Sicily Presenting Monreale Cathedral to the Virgin,* 12th Century. Monreale Cathedral. (Photo: Alinari/ Art Resource, New York.)

gain insight into the mind of the monarch whose patronage brought them into existence.

Kings need buildings for practical reasons: as places to live (along with their families and servants), to conduct business (throne rooms and council chambers come to mind), to pray and to be buried (chapels, churches, mausoleums), and we might think of other functional needs. Above and beyond the practical level, however, there is the long-recognized demand that royal edifices "speak," in some fashion, about the political power, material wealth, and artistic taste of the ruler. No potentate understood this requirement better than Louis XIV. He lived during a phase of the early modern era – called the age of absolutism by historians, the Baroque period by art historians – that was fond of grand display in the arts. The taste of the era and the ambitions of its most powerful ruler merged at a particular historical crossroad to produce an architecture that still blares forth in grandiloquent cadences, proclaiming the glory of a reign.

Builder–kings had appeared in France well before Louis XIV. From the medieval period, the names of the Frankish emperor Charlemagne (reigned 768–814), Saint Louis (Louis IX, reigned 1226–70), and Charles V (reigned 1364–80) come first to mind. The association of French rulers with important buildings is visually demonstrated in a midfifteenth-century painting (Fig. 3) (perhaps by a Flemish artist working in Paris) that places Saint Louis (far left) near a view, looking across the Seine, of the medieval Louvre (a

Figure 3. Anonymous Franco-Flemish Painter, *The Crucifixion with Saints Louis IX, John the Baptist, Denis, and Charlemagne (Altarpiece of the Parlement de Paris)*, mid-15th Century. Louvre, Paris. (Photo: Réunion des Musées Nationaux.)

royal fortress and palace), and Charlemagne (far right) before the Palais (Palace), the main medieval royal residence on the Ile de la Cité in Paris (begun several centuries after Charlemagne).

Closer to Louis XIV in time, and a direct model for royal architectural patronage on a large scale, was Francis I (reigned 1515–47), the first French king who truly was imbued with the new spirit of the Italian Renaissance. From the inception of his reign, Francis launched into architectural enterprises, creating ambitious and costly new châteaux such as Chambord. Because his court was itinerant (as in the Middle Ages), Francis needed a network of royal houses that could receive him and his entourage in suitable fashion. The medieval châteaux that he inherited were too small for his greatly enlarged household and court and old-fashioned in their style and layout. Francis I's architectural enthusiasm – a French architect of the sixteenth century called him "marvelously addicted to buildings" – was not an isolated phenomenon of his time. Indeed, contemporary early modern rulers in western Europe, such as Henry VIII in England, Charles V in Spain and his other domains, the popes in Rome, and others, all were involved in building to an unusual degree. Some of the factors that stimulated this activity were the same as in France: enlarged households, bureaucracies, and courts, and a desire to be seen in the ambiance of the new architectural and decorative Renaissance style. But in addition, the very gesture of ordering an edifice to be built (and paying for it) was considered, in Renaissance thought, to be the mark of the true prince. Baldassare Castiglione, who defined the new Renaissance ruler and courtier in his much-read *The Courtier* (finished in 1516, first published in 1528), put the following words in the mouth of one of his speakers:

I should also try to induce him [the prince] to build great edifices, both to win honor in his lifetime and to leave the memory of himself to posterity: as Duke Federico [da Montefeltro] did in the case of this noble palace [the Ducal Palace, Urbino], and as Pope Julius [II] is now doing in the case of St. Peter's Church [in Rome] and that street [actually the Belvedere Court] which leads from the [Vatican] Palace to his pleasure pavilion the Belvedere, and many other buildings: as also the ancient Romans did, whereof we see so many remains at Rome and at Naples, at Pozzuoli, at Baia, at Civita Vecchia, at Porto, as well as outside Italy, and in many other places — all of which is great proof of the worthiness of those divine minds. So Alexander the Great did also, for, not content with the fame he had rightly won by conquering the world with arms, he built Alexandria in Egypt, Bucephalia in India, and other cities in other countries; and he thought of giving Mount Athos the form of a man, and of building a very spacious city in the man's left hand and in his right a great basin in which were to be gathered all the rivers that rise there, and these were to overflow thence into the sea: a grand thought indeed and worthy of Alexander the Great. (Book IV)

Earlier in the book, Castiglione praised Duke Federico (1422–82) — an important patron of the early Italian Renaissance — for his "prudence, humanity, justice, generosity, undaunted spirit . . . [and] military prowess." He then continued:

Among his other laudable deeds, he built on the rugged site of Urbino a palace thought by many the most beautiful to be found anywhere in all Italy and he furnished it so well with every suitable thing that it seemed not a palace but a city in the form of a palace; and furnished it not only with what is customary, such as silver vases, wall hangings of the richest cloth of gold, silk, and other like things, but for ornament he added countless ancient statues of marble and bronze, rare paintings, and musical instruments of every sort; nor did he wish to have anything there that was not most rare and excellent. Then, at great expense, he collected many very excellent and rare books in Greek, Latin, and Hebrew, all of which he adorned with gold and silver, deeming these to be the supreme excellence of his great palace. (Book I)

For Castiglione and the Renaissance, the modern ruler had to possess artistic taste and an appreciation for learning; it was not sufficient for him, as previously in the Middle Ages, to be only a warrior and lawgiver. And these new expectations were fulfilled by early modern rulers – Francis I, Henry VIII, Charles V, and before them by Italian rulers like Duke Federico da Montefeltro and by the popes from the midfifteenth century on. In the case of Francis I, he brought many eminent Italian artists to France (including Leonardo da Vinci, who died there in 1519), had his buildings decorated by them (most spectacularly, the Château of Fontainebleau), and displayed his collections of ancient statues, coins, gems, and modern works of art (the paintings of Leonardo and others, which now form the core of the Louvre collection).

Francis's example as a builder, patron, and collector was not equalled in France until Louis XIV (who then surpassed him). The reasons for this are complex, and have to do as much with political and economic conditions as with the temperaments of the individual monarchs. That is not to say that the Crown did not build and patronize the arts between Francis I and Louis XIV. Suffice it to note that there was important royal architectural activity between their reigns, particularly under Henry II (reigned 1547–59) and Henry IV (reigned 1589–1610), but the scale of such efforts increased significantly under the Sun King. And, most important, architectural style changed profoundly.

In all public gestures (which, in effect, meant in almost everything he ever did), Louis XIV sought to enhance his *gloire,* meaning his glorious reputation. In this he was like most European rulers of his day. But Louis understood better than any of the others that architecture – a medium more monumental and more durable than sculpture or painting – could play as important, or even greater, a role in ensuring *gloire* as could a military campaign or a political treaty.

In the *Mémoires for the Instruction of the Dauphin,* which the King wrote with the assistance of secretaries, he described himself in 1661, when he began his personal rule, as

wanting more than anything, even more than life itself, to acquire a great reputation if I could do so, but realizing at the same time that my first moves would either lay its foundations or would destroy my hopes for it forever, so that I was almost equally pressed and restrained in my aspirations by the same desire for glory.

It was to this pronounced sense of *gloire* that his minister Colbert appealed, in a famous letter to Louis of 1663, advising him that Versailles "concerns much more the pleasure and recreation of Your Majesty than his *gloire,*" and that it was to the neglected Louvre, a building more worthy of his greatness, that he should devote his attentions (and financial resources). In the same letter, Colbert reminded the young Monarch about the power of architecture in statecraft:

Your Majesty knows that in lieu of dazzling actions in war, nothing indicates better the greatness and spirit of princes than buildings; and all posterity measures them by the standard of these superb buildings that they have erected during their lives.

Architecture and *gloire*, then, were closely associated in the Sun King's mind from his earliest years of personal rule. *Gloire* was the driving force that impelled Louis to build much and build grandly.

Later chapters will deal with Louis' buildings in some detail as well as with his artistic taste and enthusiasm for architecture. Here it will be useful to discuss some broad currents that affected architecture during the Ludovican period.

By 1661, the year in which Louis XIV began his personal rule (preceded by the regency period, 1643–61; Chap. 2), Italian eminence in the visual arts, established during the Renaissance, was still conceded by the French. Italian artists were still being lured to France by the Crown, although to a lesser extent than in the days of Francis I; in Chapter 4, we shall read about Bernini's sojourn in Paris in 1665 when he was asked to design the Louvre. And yet the sands of artistic taste were shifting, as signaled by a bellwether publication of 1650, *The Parallel of Ancient and Modern Architecture* by Roland Fréart de Chambray, a critic and connoisseur. This writer believed that French art was then in a period of decline, although he looked with pride upon the contemporary French painter Nicolas Poussin (who worked almost exclusively in Rome), whom he called "the honor of the French in his profession and the Raphael of our century." In the *Parallel*, Fréart de Chambray expressed high admiration for the Italian Renaissance architect Andrea Palladio (1508–80) (Fig. 130), declaring him to be the greatest modern architect and recommending his works as models. Fréart was highly critical of seventeenth-century architecture in France, and, significantly, even more so of recent Italian work:

Finally one can say that poor Architecture is badly treated. But one must not impute the greatest criticism to our French workers; because the Italians are now more licentious, and well reveal that Rome has at the present time her moderns as well as her ancients.

This new willingness to criticize the Italians is a symptom of a growing artistic confidence in France. The reign of Louis XIV was precisely the time when French art – particularly the royal architecture – attained an international stature equal to Italian work. This came about relatively early

Figure 4. Jean Warin, *Louis XIV*, 1665–6. Musée National du Château de Versailles. (Photo: Réunion des Musées Nationaux.)

Figure 5. Gianlorenzo Bernini, *Louis XIV*, 1665. Château, Versailles, Salon of Diana. (Photo: Réunion des Musées Nationaux.)

during the King's personal rule with the creation of the Louvre Colonnade, a building of startling aesthetic and engineering originality and a rebuke to Bernini's rejected projects (Chap. 4). And yet throughout our period, contemporary Italian art continued to fascinate the French, resulting in rivalrous and often ambivalent attitudes. Rivalry is clearly expressed in an item published in the *Gazette de France* (France's first newspaper) in 1666, which relates that

The King came . . . to see . . . a marble bust [carved 1665–6] that the sieur [Jean] Warin has made of His Majesty [Fig. 4], who highly praised this beautiful work, as did all the seigneurs who accompanied him, judging thereby that France possesses in the fine arts men as great as can be found elsewhere.

The last remark is probably a reference to Bernini and, by implication, to his bust of the King carved the year before (Fig. 5); the two effigies were later displayed in the Château of Versailles, Warin's in the staircage, Bernini's in a nearby room (where it remains), thus continuing this little competition.

Fréart de Chambray's passage quoted earlier also presages an important theme running through our period, the extent to which ancient prototypes, architectural or otherwise, should be followed by contemporaries. Here we must pause to reflect upon the fact that the core curriculum for better-educated French youth in seventeenth-century France was Greek and Latin grammar and literature. In Molière's *The Imaginary Invalid*, first performed in 1673, Thomas, a pompous suitor seeking the hand of Angélique, intersperses his little speeches with Latin phrases and reminds her how, in ancient times, it was customary for the men to carry off the young women by force. To which Angélique deftly replies:

Les anciens, monsieur, sont les anciens, et nous sommes les gens de maintenant. (II.6)

(The ancients, monsieur, are the ancients, and we are the people of the here-and-now.)

Molière was clearly for the moderns; Fréart's sympathies lay mainly with the ancients, who for him were the Greeks and those ancient Roman architects who followed Greek practice. Ancient architecture – mainly known in the form of Roman architecture (many remains of which are strewn throughout France) – was a constant referent in the Ludovican age, to be followed, violated, or simply ignored. The literary phase of the debate, known as the Quarrel of the Ancients and Moderns, was initiated in 1687 when Charles Perrault (the brother of an architect we shall meet later) had a long poem read to the French Academy called "The Century of Louis the Great," which extolled the Moderns. Well before that date, however, the question was being argued by architectural theorists (from the early 1670s on). Another issue of concern during the age of Louis XIV was the concept of "decorum" (in French, *convenance* or *bienséance*) in the arts, by which was meant, in architecture, the suitability of form to purpose or function. For example, a stable for horses should not resemble a domestic dwelling. The concept was also applied to parts and details of buildings. Thus, the floor of a château on which the owner lived should somehow be distinguished on the exterior by more monumental or richer articulation than that given to the other stories. We shall discover in the edifices of Louis XIV a surprising range of architectural and decorative expression, from the florid (Versailles, Galerie des Glaces, Fig. 96) to the austere (Versailles, Orangerie, Figs. 88 and 89). These variations, usually interpreted by architectural historians as changes in a particular architect's developing style, are in some instances better understood as responses to the demands of decorum.

The era of Louis XIV – France's golden age of culture and the arts – looked upon the classical tradition (the tradition extolled by Fréart de Chambray) as the secure pathway to beauty. Nevertheless, there continued to be an interest in the medieval past, as well as a new curiosity about distant, exotic realms, particularly China. Much of the concern with the Middle Ages was of an antiquarian and local nature, typically found among provincial clergy engrossed in tracing the history of their church or parish. However, the aesthetic power and structural daring of medieval buildings, particularly those in the Gothic style (which still abound throughout France), affected some architects and writers on architecture, with some consequences for the royal buildings of the Sun King. As for exotic, specifically Chinese, influences, here, too, some surprising instances will be discussed. The developing interests in, especially, the Gothic and China were preludes to the greatly expanded fascination with these and other nonclassical traditions that was to flourish during the eighteenth century.

* * *

The royal enterprises to be discussed in the following chapters will abundantly testify to the central importance of architecture during the Sun King's reign. His buildings, gardens, urban initiatives, and military constructions provided for the practical and symbolic needs of himself, his family, court, government, and subjects. From the onset of his personal reign in 1661 until almost his last days in 1715, Louis XIV was an unusually active and involved patron of the building arts. Patronage (whether architectural or any other kind) is a term that can cover a broad spectrum of involvement. At its most basic and passive, patronage involves support, in some form, for the project at hand, usually by the provision of funds. Some patrons, however, take a somewhat more active role: a scheme is submitted to them for their approval, or they may decide between alternate, competing proposals. Louis XIV was a patron in all these senses: he provided the necessary funds from the Crown treasury; he approved specific designs; and he sometimes established architectural competitions and chose the winning project. Architectural decision making was never delegated; all projects had to meet with his approval before they were set in motion. This in itself was not exceptional among rulers of the early modern period. What was unusual was the King's close and continuous attention to all details of design and the progress of construction. Certainly, the details of design often called for his aesthetic responses, and there can be little doubt that Louis enjoyed architecture as an artistic medium, just as he delighted in painting and sculpture, opera, ballet, and drama. In supporting the arts, the King acted as liberal benefactor and connoisseur, roles expected of all monarchs from the time of the Renaissance.

The first step in the architectural process was the recognition of a need (for a new château, a long gallery in an existing building, a fountain at a particular garden site, and so on). This might have begun in the King's mind

Figure 6. Office of Jules Hardouin-Mansart, Studies for Windows for the Main Floor of the Envelope, Château of Versailles. Drawing, 1678/9. Archives Nationales, Paris. (From A. Marie and J. Marie, *Mansart à Versailles*, II, Paris, 1972.)

or have been suggested to him by his building superintendent or other influential members of the court and government (the artistic bureaucracy will be discussed in Chap. 3). A program was then articulated and communicated to the architect, either verbally or in written form. The latter then prepared drawings, sometimes with the help of assistants, that were shown to the superintendent, who discussed them with the King (sometimes in the presence of the architect). These drawings (which have survived in great abundance) frequently show alternative proposals for the Monarch to choose from. Figure 6 is a drawing of 1678/9 from Jules Hardouin-Mansart's office for the exterior windows of the main floor of the Envelope of Versailles, undergoing revision because of the construction of the Galerie des Glaces (Chap. 10). Six variants are delineated, including the window of the original, then extant design (third from right). The window second from the right is borrowed from the ground floor of the Louvre; the fourth from the right has a depressed arch; and the remaining three show variants all with semicircular arches. The King chose the design at the far left, which leaves a space between the crown of the arch and the architrave above, with the spandrels filled with trophies. In the executed building, the space above the crown is occupied by a helmet, and the keystone is marked by a swag of drapery or armor. Close examination of Mansart's drawing reveals some touches around the keystone that adumbrate the executed design, marks that may have been added by the architect when discussing the drawing with Jean-Baptiste Colbert (the superintendent) and the King. Similar drawings abound for many of the royal projects.

Architectural drawings and memoranda were dispatched to Louis XIV even when he was on military campaigns, as was the case during 1674–5 with successive designs for the Château of Clagny (Chap. 8). In 1672, when asked by Colbert whether he preferred short or long written reports about the progress of construction, the King replied: "Long ones. Details about everything." Surviving letters to the King from Colbert and the later superintendents frequently bear marginal comments in Louis' hand (among them, the one just quoted). We can easily imagine him taking delight in examining the wood or plaster models that were sometimes built, as in the case of the Louvre and the Observatoire (Chaps. 4 and 5), as well as the *plans-reliefs* (Figs. 143 and 146). And the final adjustments of a work *in situ* could be subject to the King's judgment, as in 1677 when the English philosopher John Locke observed Louis in the gardens of Versailles:

The king seemed to be mightily well pleased with his water works and severall changes were made then to which he himself gave sign with his cane. . . .

Louis' thorough engagement with architecture, however, bespeaks a special passion for that art, and begs the question of whether, in some instances, he acted as his own architect. This problem will be explored in Chapter 14.

THE REGENCY (1643–1661)

Louis XIV was not yet five years old when he succeeded to the French throne in 1643 upon the death of his father, Louis XIII. His younger brother, Philippe, had been born in 1640. Their mother, Anne of Austria (a Spanish princess) was appointed Regent, but the real political power during the regency period was in the hands of the first minister, Jules Cardinal Mazarin (1602–61).

Mazarin was an Italian, born Giulio Mazarini. Jesuit-educated with a degree in law, he led successive careers as soldier, diplomat, and papal nuncio to the French court (1634–6). In 1639, he became a naturalized citizen of France and served as a diplomat for Cardinal Richelieu, Louis XIII's first minister. His success in this post led to his being named cardinal by Pope Urban VIII, even though he had never been ordained a priest. In 1642, upon the death of Richelieu, Mazarin became first minister.

Mazarin was one of the great art collectors of his day and a supporter of contemporary Roman Baroque art, commissioning an avant-garde church façade in Rome and bringing Italian artists to Paris. (We should also note that Mazarin was an opera lover, and introduced Italian opera to the French capital in 1645.) He failed in his efforts to entice Bernini, but succeeded in the case of Giovanni Francesco Romanelli, who introduced an Italian Baroque interior decorative style in the cardinal's house in Paris, the Palais Mazarin (1646–7, Fig. 7) and in Anne of Austria's summer apartment in the Louvre (1654–7, Fig. 8), where he was assisted by Italian and French sculptors who provided the stucco figures and moldings that accompany the frescoes, creating a rich and complex ensemble. It is tempting to ascribe Louis XIV's later activities as an art collector and patron, and also his taste that often favored Italian Baroque style, to Mazarin's influence and the new ceilings in his mother's Louvre apartment. This question should perhaps be kept open at present, but there is as yet no evidence that

Figure 7. Robert Nanteuil, *Cardinal Mazarin in his Gallery.* Engraving, 1659. (Photo: Bibliothèque Nationale, Paris.)

Figure 8. Giovanni Francesco Romanelli and Michel Anguier, Ceiling (detail) of the Petit Cabinet (now Salle des Antonins), Summer Apartment of Anne of Austria, Louvre, Paris, 1654–7. (Photo: Réunion des Musées Nationaux.)

Mazarin deliberately introduced Louis to these aspects of his many-sided activities.

Anne of Austria and Mazarin supervised Louis XIV's upbringing and selected his tutors. Their charge lacked an academic inclination; he did not receive a humanistic education, based on Greek and Latin, and never developed an interest in reading. The boy was, however, exposed to a broad variety of subjects, from the intellectual (arithmetic, elementary Latin) to the physical (horsemanship, fencing). Mazarin, who was Louis' godfather at his baptism, became the close confidant of Anne, and even during their lifetimes, it was rumored that they were lovers (modern historians are still undecided about this). Mazarin came to fill the role of stepfather (in deed if not in name) to the young King. He initiated Louis into the craft of kingship by including him from an early age in council meetings where governmental decisions were made. The cardinal also saw that the boy was tutored in military matters and had him spend time with the army, observing sieges along the northern border (France was at war with Spain, which controlled the southern Netherlands, from 1635 to 1659). He also took Louis along on hunting parties. Mazarin's ideas about education were practical, not bookish or aesthetic; if a boy was going to rule as a king, he should learn to do kingly things, and for Mazarin, this meant decision making, diplomacy, and war.

However, some of the subjects taught by the royal tutors were by nature artistic: drawing, music, dancing. Work in these areas must have helped the young King develop his latent aesthetic sensibilities, for as an adult he took keen pleasure, not only in the visual arts, but also in music, dance, opera, and drama. But dance was the area in which he excelled. Athletic and well-coordinated, Louis took daily lessons from a professional. He danced before the court in 1647 when he was eleven and appeared as a soloist in court ballets from 1651 to 1669; in 1661, he even founded an academy of dance (Chap. 3).

It was by performing different roles in the court ballets (*ballets de cour*) that Louis learned about classical mythology and its associations with the French monarchy. The court ballet had its origins in the sixteenth century as a royal and aristocratic entertainment in which the French kings usually performed. Combining the arts of dance, music, poetry, drama, and sometimes scenography, it featured masked and costumed dancers in usually mythological roles. Louis first appeared as the sun in the *Ballet of Night* of 1653, driving away darkness and preceded by Aurora, a dancer who declaimed:

> The troop of stars flees
> As this great star advances;

> The feeble illuminations of night
> That triumph in his absence
> Do not dare remain present:
> All these fickle fires vanish,
> The Sun who follows me is the young LOUIS.

In a court ballet of the following year, the *Marriage of Peleus and Thetis*, the sixteen-year-old again appeared as Apollo (conflated with the sun) (Fig. 9), and spoke verses directly alluding to the recent end of a civil war, the Fronde, that had threatened the powers of the monarchy:

> I have vanquished that Python who devastated the world,
> That terrible serpent whom Hell and the Fronde,
> Had seasoned with a dangerous venom:
> The Revolt, in one word, can no longer harm me;
> And I preferred to destroy it,
> Than to hasten after Daphne.

This may have been the first instance in which the Fronde was personified by the Python of mythology, henceforth to become standard in the official iconography of Louis XIV. But the theme of Apollo slaying the Python had been used as early as 1617 in royal French imagery to allude to Louis XIII's triumph over political enemies, and even before that, in the sixteenth century, the Python had appeared in French art as a personification of the Protestant heresy. And the occasional association of the French king with Apollo or the sun can be traced back to the fourteenth century.

A contemporary description of the King's Apollo costume for this ballet (Fig. 9) gives an indication of the richness and fantasy of the costumes provided for these entertainments: "The King's costume was covered with a rich golden embroidery with a quantity of rubies, the rays that appear around his head were of diamonds, and the crown that surrounds this hairdo was of rubies and pearls, laden with many flesh-colored and white feathers."

The poet who composed the texts of these and many other *ballets de cour* under Louis XIV (which encompass a wide range of mythological characters and situations) was Isaac de Benserade (1612–91). He surely consulted other court intellectuals who were trying to formulate a consistent program of visual imagery for the young Monarch. With the creation of the Petite Académie in 1663 (Chap. 3), a formal body was established to specifically address this task.

We shall see in the course of this book that classical mythology had a very real bearing not only on the decorations of Louis' buildings and gardens but at times on the architecture itself. During his minority, the King grew up, of course, with buildings all around him, visiting and living in the royal châteaux, such as the Louvre, Saint-Germain-en-Laye, Fontainebleau,

Figure 9. Anonymous French Painter, *Louis XIV Dancing the Role of Apollo,* 1654. MS, Bibliothèque de l'Institut de France, Paris. (Photo: Photographie Bulloz.)

and the others. Religious services brought him often within medieval settings, and his coronation in 1654 took him, by tradition, within one of the great Gothic masterpieces, Reims cathedral, but he also knew Notre-Dame in Paris. We do not know what he thought then about these structures. During these years, he journeyed within the kingdom, where he was able to observe, if he was in the least interested, the many different styles encompassed by French architecture. Additionally, in 1659–60, Louis traveled through the southern half of France (via Bordeaux) to the Spanish border to wed the Infanta, Maria-Teresa, the daughter of Philip IV of Spain. In the course of this tour, he visited the well-preserved ancient Roman ruins of Provence. Of the rear elevation of the theater at Orange, he is said to have exclaimed, "It is the most beautiful wall in my kingdom." This architectural experience in Provence must have left indelible memories. Much later in his reign, his huge but never-completed aqueduct at Maintenon (intended to bring water to Versailles and Marly; Fig. 93) must have been intended to rival the Pont du Gard.

Louis grew up knowing that he was a king (those who attended him were always deferential, even his younger brother); he knew, too, from an early age that French kings were builders and that architecture would be one of his responsibilities. No one, however, could have foretold, even at the end of his minority, that he would rapidly become one of the greatest architectural patrons in history.

3

THE EARLY YEARS OF PERSONAL RULE
The King and Colbert (1661–1671)

Cardinal Mazarin died on March 9, 1661. The very next day, the King, not yet twenty-three years old, announced that he would not appoint another first minister, but would govern by himself. That meant that all government decisions, including of course anything having to do with building, would have to pass his personal scrutiny.

At Mazarin's death, Louis inherited a royal building administration (concerned with finances and general oversight), headed by Antoine de Ratabon, superintendent since 1656. He also was bequeathed Louis Le Vau, first architect since 1654. The latter had been privately employed, since 1656, by the finance minister, Nicolas Fouquet, in building his Château of Vaux-le-Vicomte (Fig. 10). Le Vau was assisted in this major commission by Charles Le Brun (soon to be first painter) and the royal garden designer André Le Nôtre. With Vaux almost finished in 1661, Fouquet foolishly invited the King to attend a lavish *fête* there in August. Here could be seen, on a grand scale, the very latest in French architecture, interior decoration, and garden design. The château itself, composed of separately roofed pavilions in the French tradition, features a monumental two-story, domed salon, oval in plan, projecting toward the garden. Le Brun's interiors display painted illusionistic ceilings, massive gilded moldings, and wall panels painted with arabesques. Le Nôtre's garden is filled with spectacular features, such as a canal, grotto, and a distant vista breaking through the garden confines to the top of a hill. Above all, there was established a new unity between the château and its garden. However, the scale and quality of the entire design, and the specific motif of the dome, were royal, not ministerial gestures, and thereby did Fouquet overstep prudent bounds, as did his personal motto "Quo non ascendam" (Whither shall I not ascend?).

Less than a month after the *fête* of Vaux, Fouquet was arrested by the Crown, the victim of the machinations of Jean-Baptiste Colbert (1619–83),

Figure 10. Louis Le Vau and André Le Nôtre, Château and Garden of Vaux-le-Vicomte, 1656–61. (Photo: Giraudon/Art Resource, New York.)

Mazarin's assistant, newly appointed by the King as intendant of finances under Fouquet. Even before the *fête*, Louis, alerted by Colbert, had become alarmed about Fouquet's fortification of an island off the west coast of France; the ostentation of Vaux only confirmed royal suspicions of financial malfeasance. The arrest of the finance minister (followed by his subsequent trial, conviction, and imprisonment in 1664) left the field clear for Colbert, who became a minister of state in 1661, replacing Fouquet in the King's council.

Vaux-le-Vicomte demonstrated to Louis and Colbert (who also had attended the *fête*) the abilities of the royal artists Le Vau, Le Brun, and Le Nôtre when they worked together as a team, with the result that this triumvirate was soon set to work in creating the new Versailles (Chap. 6).

The rise to power of Colbert in 1661 had enormous consequences for France and its royal architecture. First and foremost, Colbert set about reforming the entire financial system of the kingdom. Following mercantilist ideas, instituting protectionist policies, promoting exports, creating royal manufactories, and increasing domestic tax revenues, Colbert doubled the Crown's net income between 1661 and 1671, thus providing the King with sufficient revenues to embark on his extensive building program. The architectural initiatives of this decade were soundly funded; in later years,

Figure 11. Claude Lefebvre, *Jean-Baptiste Colbert*, 1666. Musée National du Château de Versailles. (Photo: Réunion des Musées Nationaux.)

however, the King's net revenues decreased, but he persisted in building with all his initial enthusiasm, with resulting problems when the bills fell due.

From the very start, Colbert concerned himself with the arts, and created or strengthened organs of centralized control. Appointed vice-protector of the Royal Academy of Painting and Sculpture in 1661, he succeeded in 1663 in forcing almost all court artists to join that body (founded in 1648) and initiated an educational program of analytical lectures given by the members to colleagues and students on masterpieces from the royal collections. In 1664, Colbert purchased the superintendency of the King's buildings from Ratabon (government positions could be bought and sold privately in those days), and a new era for architecture dawned in France. As superintendent, Colbert played a major role in decision making and was a direct intermediary between the King and his architects. He held that position until his death in 1683. Lefebvre's portrait of 1666 (Fig. 11) appropriately depicts the indefatigable minister associated with Atlas.

In 1663, Colbert established the so-called Petite Académie, a small group of learned literary men who were charged with the task of inventing appropriate inscriptions, in Latin and French, for royal medals and monuments. In practice, this group (which in 1701 officially was named the Royal Academy of Inscriptions and Medals) exercised an oversight over all royal projects involving the visual arts, with special concern for symbolic and allegorical meaning. For example, royal works of art (including the decora-

Figure 12. Medal, NEC PLURIBUS IMPAR, 1667. Bibliothèque Nationale, Paris, Cabinet des Médailles. (Photo: Bibliothèque Nationale, Paris.)

Figure 13. Apollo Mask. Musée de la Marine, Paris. (Photo: Musée de la Marine.)

tion of buildings) that contained images of Apollo, Hercules, or Alexander the Great (three of the Sun King's *personae*) were scrutinized by this group.

In his *Mémoires for the Instruction of the Dauphin* for 1662, Louis wrote that it was in that year that he adopted the sun as his emblem and another of the earth with the motto NEC PLURIBUS IMPAR (not unequal to many) (Fig. 12):

It was then that I adopted the [emblem] that I have retained ever since and that you see everywhere. I believed that, rather than dwelling on something private and minor, it should in some way portray the duties of a prince and always inspire me to fulfill them. Chosen as the symbol was the sun, which, according to the rules of this art, is the noblest of all, and which, by virtue of its uniqueness, by the brilliance that surrounds it, by the light that it imparts to the other heavenly bodies that seem to pay it court, by its equal and just distribution of this same light to all the various parts of the world, by the good that it does everywhere, constantly producing life, joy, and activity everywhere, by its perpetual yet always imperceptible movement, by never departing or deviating from its steady and invariable course, assuredly makes a most vivid and a most beautiful image for a great monarch.

Those who saw me managing the cares of royalty with such ease and with such confidence induced me to add the sphere of the earth, and as its motto, NEC PLURIBUS IMPAR, by which they meant to flatter the ambition of a young king, in that with all my capacities, I would be just as capable of ruling still other empires as would the sun of illuminating still other worlds with its rays. I know that some obscurity has been found in these words, and I have no doubt that the same symbol might have suggested some happier ones. Others have been presented to me since, but this one having already been used in my buildings and in an infinite number of other things, I have not deemed it appropriate to change it.

In point of fact, the sun (conflated with Apollo; Fig. 13) and the Latin motto had been used for Louis as early as the 1650s; it may well be that they were "officially" adopted only in 1662, but this would have been before the founding of the Petite Académie the next year. This indicates that this body received a certain amount of traditional symbolism that had already developed around the young Monarch, symbolism that had been recently devised or appropriated from older traditions by court intellectuals and artistic advisers (Chap. 2).

The first decade of Louis XIV's personal rule was marked by the creation of additional royal academies, which strengthened the Crown's control of the arts and sciences. The French Academy (the literary academy) had been established in 1635, and in 1648, the Royal Academy of Painting and Sculpture was founded. In 1661, the King created the Royal Academy of the Dance, an art that he himself practiced in court ballets (Chap. 2). The other new royal academies, like the Petite Académie, were due to the initiatives of Colbert: the French Academy in Rome (1666), Sciences (also 1666; Chap. 5), Music (1669, but really an opera company; musical theory was discussed in the Royal Academy of Sciences), and, last but not least, Architecture (1671), the latter being the first institution exclusively devoted to that art. In addition, in 1662, Colbert established the Gobelins manufactory on the Left Bank in Paris, placing it under Le Brun's direction the next year; it was here that de luxe decorative furnishings (such as tapestries and metal objects) for the royal châteaux and for export were created (Fig. 14).

Colbert was probably thinking of an architecture academy as early as 1662, as is suggested by a notation on a plan by Le Vau. It is unclear why he waited until the last day of 1671 to formally convene that institution. He appointed as director the mathematician and architect François Blondel, a member of the new Royal Academy of Sciences. As a practicing architect, Blondel has left his mark principally in the area of Parisian urbanism (Chap. 7). Blondel was joined in the Academy by six members, including some architects whom we will meet later (Libéral Bruant, Chap. 9; Daniel Gittard, Chap. 12; Antoine Le Pautre, Chap. 8; François Le Vau, Chap. 4; and François d'Orbay, Chap. 6). (The other charter member was Pierre Mignard, not to be confused with his namesake and relative, the famous painter. As for Louis Le Vau, he had died in 1670, and his position of first architect was left unfilled until eleven years later, when Jules Hardouin-Mansart was appointed to the post.)

The director and members received annual stipends from the Crown. The tasks of the Academy included lectures by the director to students twice a

Figure 14. Gobelins Tapestry, *Visit of Louis XIV and Colbert to the Gobelins, 1667,* woven 1673–9. Mobilier National, Paris. (Photo: Mobilier National.)

week (those by Blondel were eventually published); there were also weekly meetings of the academicians to discuss aesthetics and specific architectural questions; to read and comment on architectural treatises (Alberti, Palladio, and so on); to serve as consultants and hear specific complaints concerning ongoing building projects; and, occasionally, to make site visits to buildings and quarries (as the Academy did in 1678, drawing up a report on building stones). In 1676, the King's Council of State decreed that the title architect of the king (*architecte du roi*) – a title liberally appropriated in former years by architects unconnected to the Crown, and even by contractors and masons – could only be used by members of the Royal Academy of Architecture. (In practice, after that date, a nonmember architect who worked on royal projects was called an *architecte ordinaire des bâtiments du roi*, an ordinary architect of the king's buildings.) The number of members gradually increased over the years, and in 1699, two categories of membership were established, royal architects and experts in construction. Beginning in 1667, promising architectural students were sent to study in Rome for three years at the newly established French Academy. There, along with prizewinners in painting and sculpture, they would lead a rigorous existence (their days began at 5 A.M.), studying architecture, arithmetic, geometry, perspective, and drawing the famous ancient ruins of the Eternal City. Upon returning to France, these students would be ready to begin working careers leading to the status of *architecte du roi*.

By 1672, then, Louis XIV had in place a formidable centralized system (one is tempted to say a bureaucracy) for the service of architecture (as well as of painting and sculpture); an apparatus of this scope and organization had never previously been seen in history. It continued to exist, with modifications, until the French Revolution.

Much in this system was essentially traditional. The basic structure of a royal building administration headed by a superintendent, under which was a first architect (with his assistants) had been inherited from previous reigns. The Petite Académie was in a sense the institutionalization of earlier, informal presences at French courts of artistic advisers, particularly learned savants. The Academy of Architecture, however, was a new component, and it is interesting to note that it functioned with critical freedom, not hesitating to reprove royal buildings (and by implication the King's taste). For example, Blondel censured (in lectures and in print) the coupled columns of the Louvre Colonnade (Fig. 23), and in 1685, the Academy criticized the decorations of Perrault's Arc de Triomphe du Trône (Fig. 59) as suitable for festival (i.e., temporary) constructions, not for a monument intended to eternalize the King's *gloire*.

How did the system actually function under the Sun King? By putting together scattered evidence, it may be said that it operated in a flexible, not a rigid, manner. With reference to our main concern in this book – the King's buildings – it was only occasionally that the Academy of Architecture was approached to render its opinion about such projects. This was the case, for instance, with the Versailles chapel (Chap. 10; Figs. 113 and 114). The Petite Académie, on the other hand, must have been almost always consulted with regard to large decorative schemes of painting and sculpture. This was definitely the case concerning the Galerie des Glaces at Versailles (Fig. 96); an early history of the Petite Académie states that Le Brun, the painter, consulted one of its members, the Abbé Tallemant, who "furnished Monsieur Le Brun with everything that he needed, the memoirs of the King's life with such exactitude as was demanded, the coats-of-arms of the cities and the princes, etc. He devised the descriptions of the paintings and the inscriptions." As for architecture itself, we shall see how, for example, the Petite Académie in 1692 defined the underlying program for Marly (after the fact, to be sure) and invented a Latin motto for it (Chap. 11); and the group surely must have played an advisory role in connection with the Louvre Colonnade, with its display of columns inspired by Ovid (Chap. 4).

The superintendents of the royal building administration (Colbert and his successors) were intermediaries between the King and the first architects, with whom André Le Nôtre (royal gardener until his retirement in 1693) worked closely. But there was no rigid *modus operandi*, and Louis on occasion dealt directly with his designers. The latter were typically present when their presentation drawings and three-dimensional models were displayed for His Majesty's approval.

Between 1699 and 1702, the King had a register kept of his orders concerning Versailles to Mansart, who in the former year had become superintendent in addition to his role as first architect (he continued to wear both hats until his death in 1708). The dated entries are fully detailed, testifying to Louis XIV's close scrutiny of his beloved residence. His orders deal not only with the château and gardens, but also with the town (Chap. 6). Two entries from 1699 concerning town roofs and pavements epitomize the Sun King's unflagging engagement with architecture – even with its utilitarian aspects – throughout his long reign:

The King has ordered that all private persons who have houses, shacks [*baraques*], and in general any kind of building covered with tile, thatch, boards, or shingles that are within the broad limits of Versailles and the deer park [a quarter in Versailles] shall have them covered with slate. [February 23]

The King has ordered that all private persons of the town of Versailles shall be obligated to pave in front of their houses that which is unpaved. And those who have paved must renew and maintain their paving. His Majesty will have the roads maintained and renewed. [February 27]

*   *   *

Before we move on to consider Louis XIV's initial engagement with architecture during the decade following his assumption of personal rule, something must be said about the problems that beset the historian when he tries to discover the King's actual role as patron in any given instance. Readers familiar with the source materials of the Louis XIV period know that the era is very richly documented indeed. In the area of architectural history alone, we have the complete account books of the royal building administration from 1664 to 1715; the papers of the superintendents, many annotated by the King; letters and memoranda of Louis XIV himself; building estimates, contracts, and inventories; discussions of the building arts and descriptions of buildings in treatises, guidebooks, poems, and other forms; diaries and letters by numerous contemporaries; the minutes of the Royal Academy of Architecture from its founding in 1671 (and the list goes on). This mass of written material is supplemented by a plethora of original drawings, which grant insight into the working out of a design, and engravings, many with informational captions. And of course there are the extant buildings, gardens, and urban features, in varying states of preservation. This material permits the historian, in most cases, to very accurately date the royal enterprises and understand their construction history. Yet despite this embarrassment of riches, the precise role of the Monarch is often difficult to uncover. We know from Chapter 1 that it was he who ultimately gave approval to all executed projects. But it was one thing for His Majesty to have given the nod to a drawing or model submitted for royal consideration; it was another to have first formulated the idea for the scheme, or to have suggested a specific solution. For example – and to anticipate consideration of a building discussed in Chapter 6 – in 1670 a garden pavilion known as the Porcelain Trianon (Fig. 56) was built at Versailles, the last design by the first architect, Louis Le Vau, who died that year. This building was conceived by Le Vau and accepted by the court, apparently in all seriousness, as "Chinese" in style. Its architectural and decorative features will be discussed later. Here the question concerns the role of Louis XIV in the invention of this curiosity. Was it the King who first conceived the idea? If so, why? If not, who did? (And again, why?) The concept (we are tempted to say whim) of a "Chinese" pavilion could, theoretically, have first arisen in the mind of Le Vau, or Colbert, or some other member of the royal family, court, or artistic bureaucracy. We happen to know that in that very year, 1670, a French translation of a Latin book on China was published, dedicated to the French war minister, the Marquis de Louvois. Was it the Marquis who, flattered by the dedication and perhaps awakened to the mysterious East, suggested to the King (or to Colbert, or to someone) that something Chinese (perhaps, to wit, a pavilion) was just what Versailles needed? But then, if the Porcelain Trianon was not Louis XIV's idea, did he make any subsequent decisions determining its siting, function, plan, elevations, or decorative details? Were any of its features the result of his suggestions? The reader will have noticed that, because we apparently lack hard, documentary information about these matters, we have reached the brink of the slippery slope of historical speculation. The impulse to speculate about things and events is a human instinct that can no more be suppressed in the historian than in life itself. But a too rapid joyride down that slope, although often a heady experience, is fraught with risks and perils if we accept that the basic mission of the historian is the reconstruction of "what really happened." The keys for the historian must be awareness of and respect for primary evidence, coupled with prudence and common sense. In the following chapters, Louis XIV's role as a patron of architecture, with special attention to his decision making, will be explored. Hard, available evidence will guide this undertaking; speculation at some points will be inevitable, but cautious.

THE LOUVRE AND TUILERIES

Of all of Louis XIV's châteaux, the Louvre in Paris had the most venerable history, dating back to the end of the twelfth century. Most of what was standing in 1661, when Louis XIV began his personal reign, had been built in the sixteenth and earlier seventeenth centuries, but the work was unfinished. The young King's first effort there involved interior decoration, the replacement of a gallery of portraits of French kings and queens (burnt in 1661) with one concerned with the power of the sun, called the Gallery of Apollo (Fig. 15). The new decoration was devised by the first painter, Charles Le Brun; the contracts were signed in May 1663, three months after the founding of the Petite Académie (Chap. 3), suggesting that the gallery was the first major royal project in which the Petite Académie played an advisory role.

The Gallery of Apollo is an example of a long gallery, a type of room impressive for its dimensions, perspective view, and rich decoration in the form of painted walls and/or ceiling. Found in French architecture of the fifteenth and sixteenth centuries, it served as the *pièce de résistance*, calculated to bedazzle the visitor.

Le Brun's decorations fill the long barrel vault and the two lunettes at the ends of the room. The vault surface is complexly divided into a variety of painted compartments that are accompanied by high relief stucco sculpture (executed by several artists). We have seen this formula used in the earlier apartments of Anne of Austria in the Louvre (Fig. 8), but in Le Brun's design, the sculpture takes on higher relief. The framing elements and sculpture, along with the abundant use of gilding, transform the vault into a resplendent armature for paintings celebrating Apollo's life-giving force, a metaphor for the reign of the Sun King. The passage of time, with which the sun is linked, is indicated along the lower part of the vault, where appear twelve painted roundels with the labors of the months and stucco herms

Figure 15. Charles Le Brun, Gallery of Apollo, Louvre, Paris, 1663–77 (Photo: from L. Hautecoeur, *Le Louvre et les Tuileries de Louis XIV,* Paris and Brussels, 1927.)

with the signs of the zodiac. The central painting was to have depicted Apollo in the heavens in his chariot, and the end lunettes display the power of the sun on the earth (*Cybele Rejoicing at the Arrival of Dawn*) and the sea (*The Triumph of Neptune and Amphitrite*). Other paintings show Diana (the moon) and Morpheus, god of dreams, inhabitants of the realm of night that Apollo dispels. Le Brun, because of his manifold projects for Louis XIV, was often called away from this work, which was left unfinished in 1677 (it was "completed" in the eighteenth and nineteenth centuries). Nevertheless, the Galerie d'Apollon immediately became the most magnificent room in the vast palace, proclaiming the glory of the new reign.

Upon assuming personal rule in 1661, the King inherited the ongoing completion of the core of the Louvre – the Square Court – under the first architect, Le Vau. The latter's south wing facing the Seine had been begun in 1660 and was brought to completion in 1663 without any interference from the Crown (Fig. 16). For the sake of continuity with the old, esteemed Renaissance Louvre, Le Vau merely repeated the end pavilion and outer elevation of Pierre Lescot's design, but introduced a new note in a central pavilion with a columnar Corinthian order two stories high (a so-called "colossal" order) and a high pedimented attic, the pavilion covered with a four-sided French dome to match Jacques Lemercier's Pavillon de l'Horloge (Clock Pavilion, finished 1641) overlooking the Square Court. At the same time that this new south wing was being built, Le Vau's new eastern, entrance wing was also starting to rise. The first architect had turned to this part of the Louvre ca. 1659, evolving a design that eventually reached (end of 1663) a bold and original form (Fig. 17). Although it preserved the pavilion system of the older parts of the Louvre, Le Vau's wing – this time with a colossal order along its entire length – featured a curved central pavilion with a domed oval vestibule within, open to the sky, its upper part appearing on the exterior as a drum-without-dome. On January 1, 1664, Colbert, upon assuming the post of superintendent of the King's buildings, suddenly halted all work on this wing. The minister's motivations for this action – which must have received the approval of the Monarch – were probably complex, but surely an important factor contributing to his decision was the bizarre, although visually striking, quality of Le Vau's design. The drum-without-dome could be interpreted as an incomplete form, and the large open oculus above the vestibule – probably intended to introduce sunlight in a dramatic fashion as a metaphor for the Sun King – could be objected to as a funnel for precipitation. In any event, construction was stopped and Colbert invited French architects to submit new designs, in effect an open competition that was extended to four Roman architects to whom Le Vau's aborted design was sent.

Of the French projects of 1664, the most important were two: one (exhibited anonymously and not extant) by a Parisian physician and scientist named Claude Perrault, which is supposed to have featured a colonnade in some form; and a second, which has survived, by Louis Le Vau's younger brother François, begun ca. 1662 and finished by December 1664 (Fig. 18). Well before the end of that year, however, Colbert had received the Italian designs, including one by Gianlorenzo Bernini, Europe's most famous living sculptor and architect. His proposal (Fig. 19) retained the colossal order and drum-without-dome of Le Vau, but opened up the bays between the end pavilions as loggias and created a pronounced concave–convex contrast. Colbert objected in polite terms to the loggias, which he judged inappropriate for the Parisian climate, and faulted the drum-without-dome as an incorrect representation of the French royal crown (!). A second design received in March 1665 that omitted the central convex pavilion and its upper termination did not please either, but Colbert was intent on bringing the sixty-seven-year-old artist to Paris to study the situation at the Louvre in person. After a progress through France suitable for a prince, the cavaliere arrived in Paris in June 1665, staying there until late October. It was during

Figure 16. Louvre, Paris, South Façade by Louis Le Vau, 1660–3. Engraving by Jean Marot. (Photo: Houghton Library, Harvard University.)

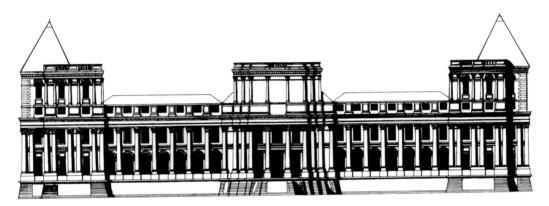

Figure 17. Louis Le Vau, Design for the East Façade of the Louvre, 1663–4. Reconstruction by Trevor K. Gould. (From *Revue de l'art*, 1969.)

this sojourn that he carved the superb marble bust of the King (Fig. 5) that was eventually set up in the Salon of Diana at Versailles (Fig. 55).

A remarkable record of this visit, the diary of Paul Fréart de Chantelou, contains eyewitness accounts of Louis XIV's interest in and reaction to Bernini's final Louvre projects. For example:

We [Chantelou and Bernini] went to Saint-Germain-en-Laye with M. Colbert. The Cavaliere [Bernini] presented his plan for the Louvre and the design for the elevation of the façade [Fig. 20]. The whole pleased His Majesty so much that he told the Cavaliere how very glad he was that he had begged the Pope to allow him to come. The King noticed among other features the rock-like base on which the Louvre was to rest; this was covered by a sheet of paper with a drawing showing this story rusticated, as an alternative because the rock would be difficult to execute. The King considered both carefully and said that he liked the rocky effect very much and asked for it to be carried out. The Cavaliere explained that he had drawn the alternative because he was afraid that the entirely novel idea of the rock might not please, but also because if it was to be carried out in accordance with his intention he himself would have to do it. The King repeated that he was extremely impressed by the rock design. To this the Cavaliere answered that it was a great pleasure to see what a delicate and discriminating taste the King had, there being few, even among the profession, who would have decided so judiciously. The King asked him also to make a design for the façade facing the service courtyard, to which he agreed and then withdrew.

On leaving we went into the chapel where the Cavaliere remained a long time in prayer, from time to time kissing the floor.

And:

As soon as the Cavaliere came in, he showed His Majesty his design for the riverside façade [Fig. 21]. The King studied it and had it explained to him and then showed it to the duc de Saint-Aignan, who was present, and to others. The King then

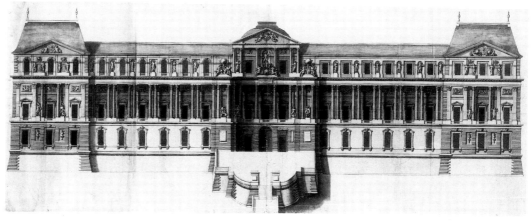

Figure 18. François Le Vau, Design for the East Façade of the Louvre. Drawing, ca. 1662–4. Nationalmuseum, Stockholm. (Photo: Statens Konstmuseer.)

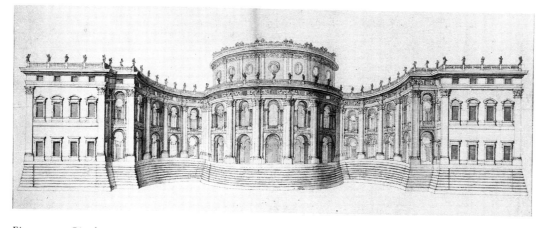

Figure 19. Gianlorenzo Bernini, Design for the East Façade of the Louvre. Drawing, 1664. Louvre, Paris, Cabinet des Dessins. (Photo: Réunion des Musées Nationaux.)

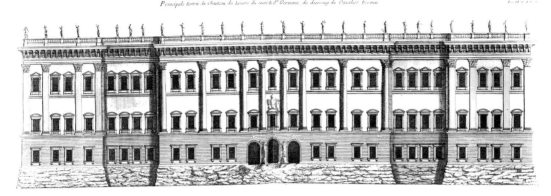

Figure 20. Gianlorenzo Bernini, Design for the East Façade of the Louvre, 1665. Engraving by Jean Marot. (Photo: Houghton Library, Harvard University.)

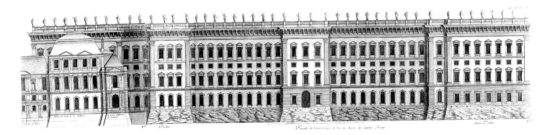

Figure 21. Gianlorenzo Bernini, Design for the South Façade of the Louvre, 1665. Engraving by Jean Marot. (Photo: Houghton Library, Harvard University.)

wanted to see it beside the façade for the front of the Louvre [Fig. 20], and asked me to hold them together, so that he could see the effect of the angle made by the two new façades. He looked at them hard. . . .

At a later time, Bernini and Chantelou judged that Louis XIV also would be interested in construction materials:

Just as His Majesty was going out, the Cavaliere showed him a bit of mortar from the Provost's Tower of the Hôtel de Ville which, he said, was of excellent quality and made with river sand. Then I told the King about the two walls that were being erected at the Palais Mazarin as a test of the comparative strength of the French and Roman methods.

His Majesty stopped for a moment to watch M. Mattia [de' Rossi, Bernini's assistant] and asked me what he was working at. I replied that he was trying to lower the height of the main floor in the elevation of the façade of the Louvre in pursuance of M. Colbert's instructions, so that it should be more suitable to the French climate. Then the Cavaliere presented to him two Italians, whom he had sent for from Rome: one was a stone cutter, the other a master mason. His Majesty asked what they would do at the Louvre. I said, "Follow their profession, and further, see that the work was carried out according to the wishes of the Cavaliere." Then the King left, saying, "Tomorrow, at the same time."

Bernini's highly favorable opinion about the French Monarch's artistic taste and judgment, given in the previous first extract, was repeated on other occasions. Although flattery was certainly at work in these instances, there is no reason to doubt that the Italian was sincere in discerning in the King something of the qualities of the connoisseur:

His Majesty [Bernini said] had noticed things in his drawings which those with great knowledge of art might not have recognized. In Rome there were a good two hundred people who were concerned with architecture; he would boldly assert that in this great number there would be few who would have recognized, in the way the King did, what was admirable in his designs (supposing there was that which was admirable). . . .

And:

the spirit of the King . . . received the impression of anything of really excellent quality with a remarkable facility; he [Bernini] had been astonished, at the time when he had first presented his design for the Louvre, to see how the King had appreciated its merits at once; for a knowledge of those sciences was acquired only after long study, which of course the King had never undertaken, or by being accustomed to things of beauty around one, as in Rome, where there were not only the remains of classical buildings, but also many wonderful modern works; this experience the King had not had either; on the contrary, he was surrounded by petty and fiddling designs, so that his sureness of taste was astonishing, if not miraculous.

The Louvre project that Bernini devised while in the French capital was intended to mask all the older parts of the palace – an impolitic gesture that affronted national pride. The entrance façade (Fig. 20) was entirely revised to resemble a massive Roman *palazzo*, with shallow central and end pavilions as the only bow to the French tradition. A colossal Corinthian order united the two upper floors, and the whole was terminated in Italian style by a balustrade without visible roof. The central portals were to be flanked by statues of Hercules (one of the King's *personae*) standing on a rugged rusticated basement – an allusion to the Mountain of Virtue that the mythological hero (alias Louis XIV) had climbed.

The cornerstone for the foundation of this very Italianate project was laid with royal ceremony a few days before Bernini's departure for Rome. What then ensued between late 1665 and the spring of 1667 is largely hidden from the historian's purview, but must have resembled diplomatic intrigue. A cabal, already formed against Bernini in 1665, went to work to persuade Colbert against the construction of Bernini's Louvre, probably on the grounds of both aesthetics and French national honor. This effort succeeded,

Figure 22. Office of Louis Le Vau, Design for the East Façade of the Louvre. Drawing, 1667. Louvre, Paris, Cabinet des Dessins. (Photo: Réunion des Musées Nationaux.)

and in April 1667, Colbert, with the approval of His Majesty, appointed a committee of three Frenchmen to design a new east façade for the Louvre. Bernini was officially notified of the abandonment of his project as late as July 15 of that year.

The panel of three, called the Petit Conseil, consisted of the first architect, Louis Le Vau, the first painter, Le Brun, and the physician, scientist, and fledgling architect Claude Perrault, whose name we encountered earlier. The latter had produced a Louvre design in 1664 and a utopian obelisk project in 1666, the latter brought to the attention of Colbert by Claude's younger brother, Charles, Colbert's assistant in the royal building administration. Perhaps as early as March 1667, Claude had been selected to be the architect of the astronomical observatory in Paris (the Observatoire, Chap. 5), to serve the needs of the newly founded Royal Academy of Sciences, to which he belonged. This commission, which must have been approved by Colbert, may have been the result of lobbying efforts by brother Charles, but we do not fully understand why Colbert appointed Claude to so important a group as the Petit Conseil; perhaps Claude's interest in the writings of Vitruvius, the ancient Roman architect, was already in evidence at this date and may have suggested to Colbert that he possessed ancient theoretical knowledge that could be useful. In any event, the committee went to work and presented two designs to the King in May, one without columns or pilasters and the other with a colonnade. It was the latter that was approved by Louis XIV (Fig. 22). Its striking similarity to François Le Vau's façade design of ca. 1662–4 (Fig. 18) strongly suggests that the younger Le Vau's drawing, available to his brother, was used as the basic model. In both, we find a high ground floor with tall, narrow windows serving as a podium for a main floor with ranges of coupled, free-standing columns; behind these columns are walls set back about twelve feet, so that porticoes or loggias are formed between the central and end pavilions. Both designs feature domes over the central pavilion, although in the drawing of 1667, the dome (difficult to see in Fig. 22) is set above a tall drum.

Construction of foundations for this design began during the summer of 1667. Between May 1667 and the first half of 1668, this scheme was refined into the final Colonnade (as it is called) that stands today, mainly constructed between 1667 and 1674 (Fig. 23). Whereas the drawing of 1667 is definitely from Louis Le Vau's office (and perhaps was drawn by the first architect himself), later crucial drawings are attributable to Perrault (a master draftsman), suggesting that he became the dominant designer in 1668. In the final redaction of the Colonnade, the central pavilion is broader, with four pairs of columns supporting a pediment. There is no attic and dome, and the whole unit is suggestive of an antique temple front. Each end pavilion, which in 1667 was to repeat the sixteenth-century corner pavilion of the Square Court (Fig. 16), is now adorned with a central arched opening flanked by columns and pilasters in the rhythm of an ancient Roman triumphal arch. The order throughout is Corinthian, a shift from the Composite of the 1667 drawing. The change in the order and the suggestions of temple front and triumphal arch may reflect the ideas of Roland Fréart de Chambray (Chap. 1), who was called to Paris to serve on the Petit Conseil in 1668.

The final Colonnade is reminiscent of some huge temple of ancient Greece or Rome. Its free-standing columns carrying straight entablatures, which are in part responsible for this impression, posed special technical problems. The entablatures, constructed as flat arches of a large number of small, carefully fitted stones (*voussoirs*), produce outward thrusts that can threaten the stability of the free-standing columns. To solve this problem, a revolutionary system of hidden iron tie rods and cramps was incorporated into the masonry as the building rose. Perhaps devised by Perrault in consultation with Parisian masons and ironworkers, the iron resists tensile forces threatening displacements of the columns and slips of the stones, leaving the masonry to act as it is best fitted to do: purely in compression. The tie rods are exposed in galleries within the entablature of the Colonnade to allow maintenance workers to adjust the tensions (Fig. 24). The King surely knew something about the technological bravura of the Colonnade, for he is reported to have said while looking at it, "If only Versailles could have been built like that."

In addition to the antique flavor and technological virtuosity of the

Figure 23. Louvre, Paris, Colonnade, begun 1667. (Photo: Author.)

Figure 24. Louvre, Paris, Colonnade, Tunnel within Entablature with Exposed Iron Tie Rods. (Photo: Rowland J. Mainstone.)

Figure 25. Louvre, Paris, View within Portico of the Colonnade. (Photo: Caroline Rose, Paris.)

Colonnade, the building also summoned up the image of the palace of the sun as described by the Latin poet Ovid, an image from antique literature suitable for the palace of the Sun King. Ovid had written in the *Metamorphoses* that "The palace of the sun stood high with lofty columns," followed by descriptions of its materials and decorations. As the Colonnade was rising in 1670, a poem was published in Paris by a minor writer/engraver, in which we read:

> Know that it is about you [the Louvre] that Ovid must have spoken
> When he described to us by means of learned fables
> The beauties of a palace that you make real:
> If the glare of the sun had not dazzled his eyes,
> He would have foretold to us that it was for LOUIS,
> That the great Apollo, that father of light,
> Inspired him to speak of these rich materials:
> That becomes clear in seeing this sun,
> The device of a king who has no equal
> And who cherishes so strongly that star and its images,
> That he has it depicted on his greatest works.

The last lines refer to the radiant Apollo faces placed on the ceilings of the porticoes (Fig. 25). In the new Louvre as built, allusions to Apollo replaced the images of Hercules proposed by Bernini (Fig. 20).

If we survey the history of earlier projects for the east façade of the

Louvre from the beginning of the seventeenth century on, we will find that designs featuring prominent columnar displays only began in 1661, very shortly after Le Brun devised a project for the cupola of Vaux-le-Vicomte. This has come down to us in a drawing (Fig. 26) in which Ovid's sun palace is shown as a broad arrangement of paired columns on a podium with a central pavilion. The design was never executed, due to the fall of Fouquet (Chap. 3), but it was known in high circles and seems to have influenced architectural projects for the new Louvre. It is perhaps not coincidental that Le Brun was a member of the Petit Conseil. Although the Colonnade contains porticoes that could be objected to on the same grounds that Colbert used to criticize Bernini's first two projects (Fig. 19), the minister did not condemn them, apparently realizing their inherent importance for the Ovidian allusion.

At the end of the seventeenth century, a fierce debate erupted about the authorship of the Colonnade. The argument has continued into recent times, with Claude Perrault usually given the credit. Modern analysis, however, reveals that a number of individuals played crucial roles, Perrault certainly, but also both Le Vaus and Fréart de Chambray. In a manner reminiscent of some twentieth-century architecture, the Louvre Colonnade turns out to have been the product of a truly collaborative effort, but one that did not compromise its artistic coherence.

One other important accomplishment by the committee was the design of a new south façade (1668; Fig. 27) facing the Seine and obliterating Le Vau's recently built front (Fig. 16). The new construction was meant to harmonize with the Colonnade, but the free-standing columns of the latter were replaced by single pilasters. The formula used here of a podiumlike ground floor with a colossal order above embracing two main stories – although ultimately derived from Italian sixteenth-century architecture and present in Bernini's final project (Figs. 20 and 21) – was to serve as a model for many buildings of the later seventeenth and eighteenth centuries in France and throughout Europe.

To the west of the Louvre, and linked to it by a long wing or gallery, was the Tuileries Palace, begun in 1564 under Queen Catherine de Médicis as a sort of suburban villa outside the city walls; construction was continued under Henry IV in the early seventeenth century. What Louis XIV inherited was a jumble of pavilions and wings, each with its own design and roof. In 1659, Mazarin conceived the idea that the little-used building could become the site for an opera house and an equestrian theater. Le Vau, as first architect, repeated the old architecture to form the north range, within which an Italian theater specialist, Gaspard Vigarani, designed a theater known as the Salle des Machines (a reference to the elaborate machinery that was used for special stage effects). The work, begun in 1659, progressed

Figure 26. Charles Le Brun, *Design for the Cupola of Vaux-le-Vicomte*. Drawing, late 1650s. Louvre, Paris, Cabinet des Dessins. (Photo: Réunion des Musées Nationaux.)

Figure 27. Louvre, Paris, South Façade, begun 1668. (Photo: Author.)

slowly and came to a halt with Mazarin's death in March 1661. One of Louis XIV's early architectural decisions (June 1661) was to order the renewal of activity at the Tuileries, which resulted in an inaugural performance of a ballet in the Salle des Machines in February 1662. Surprisingly, the theater was not used again until 1671(!), and then was abandoned by the King, despite his love for opera; it is probable that bad acoustics was the problem (an aspect of theater design with which architects still struggle).

With the advent of Colbert in 1664 as superintendent of the King's buildings, a new campaign of work was begun at the Tuileries, the architecture (by Le Vau) finished in 1666, its decorations (by a team of artists under Le Brun) in 1671. The building was now to be a royal residence, supplementing the Louvre, where there was major ongoing work that made occupancy difficult. Apartments for the members of the royal family, arranged as linear suites, were created in the enlarged south range, and the newly built north pavilion was intended for government offices. A new four-sided dome was erected over the central pavilion to harmonize with the Louvre (Fig. 28). Despite these changes, the Tuileries remained an old-fashioned looking building, which was to contrast starkly with the stylistically progressive new Louvre designed a few years later.

Aside from the Salle des Machines, the Tuileries of Louis XIV contained two interesting interior features. One was a new stair adjoining the central pavilion, Le Vau's replacement of the original sixteenth-century spiral stair by Philibert de l'Orme that was suspended on vaults within the pavilion itself. For this complex, essentially late-medieval type, Le Vau substituted a species known as the "imperial stair," in which one ascending straight flight doubles back in two more straight flights (or vice versa), all within a single, unified space or staircage. (Figure 29 is a rare view of Le Vau's stair, shown during a bloody incident during the French Revolution; some figures obscure the single straight flight in the center, rising from the floor below.) The imperial stair, originating in Spain in the late sixteenth century and used on a small scale in a few private Parisian houses in the seventeenth, was taken up at the Tuileries in a grander manner, an indication early in Louis' personal reign of an interest in ceremonial staircases that later culminated in the Ambassadors' Staircase at Versailles (Fig. 53). The other feature of note within the palace was the Ambassadors' Gallery (decorated 1666–70), not a long gallery meant to glorify the occupant of the building (e.g., the Galerie d'Apollon in the Louvre [Fig. 15] and the Galerie des Glaces at Versailles [Fig. 96]), but an exposition of Italian art for the study and delectation of artists and connoisseurs (occasionally, the room was used for ambassadorial receptions, with a throne placed at one end). The walls were hung with choice Italian masterpieces from the High Renaissance to the early Baroque, culled from the recently expanded royal collection, and the ceiling was covered with copies, freely arranged, by French artists of the Farnese Gallery (Rome) decorations of the Carracci (early seventeenth century). Thus, the room allowed systematic study of about one hundred years of one school of painting that was admired by the French, and supplemented the pedagogic program of the Royal Academy of Painting and Sculpture that Colbert had recently reorganized. Indeed, the program of the gallery may have been Colbert's brainchild, but if so, it had to have been approved by the King, particularly because the room directly adjoined his apartment (convenient for his private enjoyment). However, after 1676, the easel paintings on the walls were transferred to the King's Cabinet (seven rooms in the Louvre near the Gallery of Apollo) and to Versailles, where they decorated the royal apartments.

(In 1871, the Tuileries Palace was burnt during the Commune and was subsequently torn down except for the terminal north and south pavilions that, restored, still stand as the Pavillon de Marsan and the Pavillon de Flore.)

Stretching away from the Tuileries Palace toward the west is the Tuileries Garden, still one of the city's major green spaces. Laid out under Catherine de Médicis at the time the Tuileries Palace was begun, the garden was radically refashioned by André Le Nôtre between 1664 and 1679 (Fig. 30). Formerly surrounded by a high wall and separated from the palace by a road, the new garden of Le Nôtre did away with these encumbrances and opened up the garden to the building, the Seine, and the city. Silvestre's view shows the garden looking westward from an upper floor of the palace; from this vantage point, the intricate patterns of the embroidered *parterres* could be clearly seen. The central avenue leads past a near circular basin, past a far octagonal one, and then the view is opened up and continued beyond the then-city limits by straight lines of trees up rising ground to the horizon (the future Champs-Élysées). We are reminded of Vaux-le-Vicomte (Fig. 10), but here the distance is far greater. Le Nôtre created this view while at work at Versailles, where a similar vista down the Allée Royale and beyond was interpreted by a contemporary as a metaphor for royal rule (Figs. 42 and 43; see Chap. 6). Perhaps the same meaning was implied in the Parisian example. The distant tree-lined avenue led toward Saint-Germain-en-Laye and was the western equivalent of the avenue on the eastern side of the city leading from Vincennes into Paris, both elements of the new urbanism under Louis XIV (Chap. 7).

During the 1660s, decisions about the Louvre and the Tuileries were driven by Colbert, with final approval always reserved, of course, for the King. There is little doubt that in stopping Le Vau's east façade (Fig. 17),

LES PROMENADES DU PALAIS DES THUILLERIES.
Présenté à son Altesse Sérénissime Monseigneur le Prince de CONTY.

Figure 28. Tuileries Palace, Paris. Engraving by Jacques Rigaud. (Photo: Bibliothèque Nationale, Paris.)

rejecting Bernini's Louvre projects (Figs. 19–21), and finally supporting the building of the Colonnade (Fig. 23), Colbert's personal aesthetic taste, which was anti-Baroque, was of paramount importance. Did the King merely act in those instances as a royal rubber stamp, approving whatever Colbert recommended? There is reason to believe that he did, even in the case of the alternate proposals of 1667 for the Louvre façade, when Colbert chose the project without an order and Louis then overruled him and selected the one with a colonnade (Fig. 22) – a courtly gambit arranged by the minister. However, during the same decade at Versailles, Louis XIV clashed with Colbert and asserted his royal will (Chap. 6), thus starting down the path to increasing assertiveness in architectural decision making and the formation of a personal taste, which culminated in his involvement with the design of the Marble Trianon (Chap. 14).

In pondering Louis XIV's aesthetic taste (which surely evolved over the many decades of his reign), we might be tempted to simply point to his architecture for its definition. But it must always be remembered that the designs set before him for consideration and approval were the work of the creative genius of his artists – architects, garden designers, sculptors, painters – who, like all artists, followed their own inner voices. That is to say that Louis' taste was first and foremost the taste of his designers. Furthermore, these artists worked in a common artistic language, and when alter-

Figure 29. Louis Le Vau, Stair, Tuileries Palace, Paris, 1664. Engraving by Berthault after Prieur. (Photo: from Y. Christ, *Le Louvre et les Tuileries*, Paris, 1949).

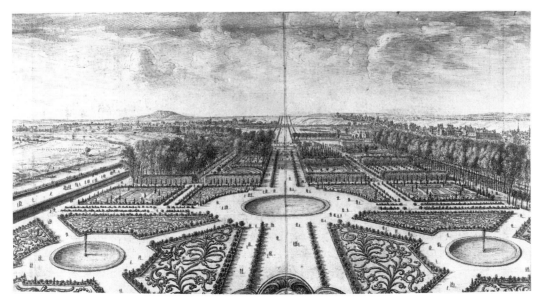

Figure 30. André Le Nôtre, Tuileries Garden, Paris, remodeled 1664–79. Drawing by Israël Silvestre. Louvre, Paris, Cabinet des Dessins. (Photo: Réunion des Musées Nationaux.)

nate designs were presented to the King for arbitration, differences between them were subtle. Determining Louis XIV's very personal *goût,* then, is not a simple matter, and only on a few occasions can it be glimpsed. These will be noted in later chapters.

A BUILDING FOR THE SCIENCES
The Observatoire

It could be argued that of all the phenomena that made up the fabric of the seventeenth century, the one that had the most profound effect on the future was the scientific revolution. Just as the dominant political system of the time – absolutism – came to be embodied in architectural form (the subject of this book), so too was a suitable permanent setting sought and achieved for the activities of early modern science. The Paris Observatoire was the first building to successfully meet this challenge.

The history of the architecture of early modern science is at first a case of new wine poured into old bottles. These first buildings were intended primarily as astronomical observatories, for astronomy was in the forefront of the new scientific thought from Copernicus on (his *De Revolutionibus Orbium Coelestium* was first published in 1543). The earliest was Tycho Brahe's Uranienborg (or Uraniborg, named after Urania, the muse of astronomy), erected on an island near Copenhagen, from 1576 to 1581 (Fig. 31, right). The building resembled a northern European castle, and, indeed, most of it served domestic functions by providing an apartment, kitchen, and library for the astronomer on the ground floor and, above, suites for the feudal lord of the island, the Danish king Frederick II, and his wife. Laboratories were in the basement, instruments for measuring time and wind direction in the crowning lantern, and astronomical observations (using Tycho's elaborate instruments, but not yet the telescope) were made from within the conical copper roofs, with openings for stargazing. Seen from a distance, Uranienborg hardly breathed the new scientific spirit in its architectural forms. (Tycho's other observatory, Stjerneborg, begun in 1580 on the same island, was completely underground.)

From the 1630s on, other "observatories" appeared across northern Europe in the forms of wooden platforms set atop older buildings. Towers

Figure 31. Astronomical Observatories of Copenhagen, Paris, and Uranienborg. Engraving from G. D. Cassini, *Divers ouvrages d'astronomie*, Amsterdam, 1736. (Photo: Houghton Library, Harvard University.)

were also erected, for example, the Round Tower (Fig. 31, left), erected in 1637 in Copenhagen under King Christian IV upon the recommendation of the astronomer Longomontanus. This was simply a seven-story tower, with a flat roof for observations and a hollow shaft within for pendulum experiments – functional, but not architecturally creative, a hoary form appropriated for new uses.

What distinguishes the Paris Observatoire (Fig. 31, center) from its predecessors is precisely that it is a building that no one could possibly mistake for a castle or a tower or anything else from traditional architecture, and in this it may be seen as embodying the contemporary theoretical demand for decorum in architecture (Chap. 1). It is the first convincing monument of the scientific revolution, and it was designed by a man of science, Claude Perrault, whom we have encountered in connection with the Louvre (Chap. 4) and who will reappear in Chapter 7 as a designer of a Parisian triumphal arch.

The Observatoire was designed and begun in 1667, and was intended to be the home of the Royal Academy of Sciences, founded at the end of the preceding year. Before 1666, French men of science had met sporadically in a number of private scientific circles in the houses of wealthy or aristocratic patrons. The continuation of these groups depended on the fortunes of the patrons; money was always an issue, and the activities of the groups tended to be unsystematic, given to verbal argumentation. In 1663, a secretary of one of these circles lamented that to build an arsenal of machines to carry out all sorts of experiments is impossible. . . . Think of the space needed for observation of the stars, and of the size of the apparatus necessary for a forty-foot telescope. . . . Was not Tycho Brahe forced to build his Uranienborg, a castle not so much for lodgings as for the making of celestial observations?

Truly, gentlemen, only kings and wealthy sovereigns or a few wise and rich republics can undertake to erect a physical academy where there would be constant experimentation. A special structure must be built to order; a number of artisans must be hired; and considerable funds are necessary for other expenses.

The French were well aware of government-sponsored scientific academies in other lands (the Accademia del Cimento in Florence, founded in 1657; the Royal Society in London, founded in 1660). They turned to Colbert, who admired systematic, rational thought but also understood the practical value of scientific work for commerce, navigation, and warfare. The nature of such an academy was debated, and in December 1666, the first meeting of the Royal Academy of Sciences was held in the King's library, housed in the rue Vivienne on the Right Bank. The members of the Academy were now salaried employees of the Crown, and thereby did they relinquish some of their former independence. In return, they received material benefits, notably in the form of scientific instruments for proceedings in which visual demonstration replaced verbal disputation. Foreigners were admitted to membership and, indeed, the first director of the Observatoire was the Italian Cassini. Only Cartesians and Jesuits were excluded, being judged not open-minded.

The selection of Perrault as architect was facilitated by his membership in the Academy and by the influence of his brother Charles, who since 1664 had been serving as Colbert's assistant in the royal building administration. More than any other building discussed in this book, the Observatoire owes its existence and spirit to Colbert. Nature had been propitious in sending forth comets in 1664 and 1665 that were visible in Paris. The scientist Adrien Auzout, in a pamphlet of 1665 about these prodigies, appealed for an observatory that would be the glory of Louis XIV and France. Colbert responded favorably, and Claude Perrault reported that in addressing the academicians after the Academy had been founded in 1666, Colbert spoke of the need for a French observatory that would surpass those of England, Denmark, and China(!). The King himself was very much aware of the enterprise. He must have approved the project when it was presented by Colbert in 1667 and he was shown Perrault's model. What the Monarch actually thought about it is not recorded, but he may have perceived that the special function of the building removed it from aesthetic yardsticks used to judge other types of structures, for instance, châteaux. Hence the austerity of the Observatoire, inside and out, could be acceptable to his undoubtedly more sumptuous taste. Two years later, the King listened to a

Figure 32. Henri Testelin, *The Founding of the Royal Academy of Sciences, 1666.* Musée National du Château de Versailles. (Photo: Réunion des Musées Nationaux.)

debate between Perrault and the newly arrived Cassini about changes in the building (then rising) that the Italian sought, changes that, according to brother Charles, were supported by Le Vau out of pique that the commission had not been given to him. Claude Perrault is said to have became so agitated during this debate that he indecorously exclaimed to Louis XIV, "Sire, this here speaker of gibberish *(baragouineur)* doesn't know what he's saying." Although the Monarch decided in favor of Perrault, Cassini's main demand, a large hall (Grande Salle) on the upper floor, was eventually built (Fig. 35).

The Observatoire was always included in contemporary lists of the King's buildings and helped disseminate the reputation of the Sun King as a protector of the sciences. An oil sketch (Fig. 32) made in preparation for a tapestry commemorating the establishment of the Royal Academy of Sciences shows Louis receiving the charter from Colbert in an imaginary setting, with the men of science gathered together and a view of the Observatoire in the background.

The Observatoire was built on the then-southern outskirts of Paris in a location judged to be free of smoke and haze for the use of the telescope and other instruments. The quality of the building that immediately attracts attention is its austerity (Figs. 33 and 34). In an age that delighted in the display of the classical orders and rich architectural decoration, the Observatoire stands out as an anomaly, a stripped-down demonstration of the stonemason's art. There are no orders – no columns or pilasters – and the decoration is confined to two reliefs of trophies of scientific instruments on the south façade (Fig. 34), the pediment on the north face (Fig. 33) filled with winged figures holding the royal arms (not extant), and a balustrade with interlaced ovals and stars at the level of the flat roof. Simple string courses demarcate the stories, and openings are either slightly recessed from the smooth wall or surrounded with barely projecting moldings. The octagonal corner towers strike an old-fashioned note, but each side was aligned with the sun's position at solstices and equinoxes (although not absolutely accurately) and the eastern one was unroofed for the use of a long telescope within.

Inside, the halls display unadorned walls flowing into vaults, with no moldings or features to mark the transitions; the architectural interest is focused on the ways the stones smoothly fit together (Fig. 35). This traditional French love of stereotomy (the art of cutting stones into shapes and figures) reaches its apex in the main stair (Fig. 36), a virtuoso display of curving ramps hung from the walls and projecting into space, with curved planes smoothly flowing together. We may be sure that Perrault, who had had no formal training or significant prior experience as an architect, worked out this display piece in close collaboration with his Parisian masons.

Louis XIV visited the Observatoire in 1682, accompanied by Queen Marie-Thérèse, their son, the Grand Dauphin, and Colbert. The Sun King was guided through the Observatoire and the visit was duly reported in the *Mercure galant* (a literary monthly that also reported news about the royal family). His Majesty gazed through telescopes; examined other scientific instruments, including a microscope; was shown a model that illustrated the rival planetary systems of Ptolemy, Copernicus, and Brahe; marveled at a painting of the moon showing its relief features; examined the publications of the academicians on animal anatomy (Perrault wrote one of these); listened to explanations of dissections; and studied a floor map of the four parts of the world. He then ascended the stair, which we are told he praised very much, halting on it for some time. The *Mercure* called it "an admirable work, both for its design which is by the famous Monsieur Perrault, as for the pattern of the stone-cutting, in which the greatest part of the beauties of that art are found in their perfection." Louis ascended to the large hall on the upper floor where the meridian of Paris was marked, along with the equinoxes and solstices. Then he climbed the stair again to the flat roof, where he must have paused for the fine view of Paris that it still affords. His attention was then led to a round opening in the center of the roof that passed through the floors below and then down a shaft running deep into the earth (the Observatoire had been built on old quarries), a shaft used for astronomical observations, experiments concerning the velocities of falling

Figure 33. Claude Perrault, Observatoire, Paris, begun 1667. Section and North Elevation. Engraving from Claude Perrault, trans. and ed., *Les dix livres d'architecture de Vitruve*, Paris, 1673. (Photo: Houghton Library, Harvard University.) *left*

Figure 34. Claude Perrault, Observatoire, Paris, begun 1667. South Façade. (Photo: Collection Viollet.) *below*

Figure 35. Claude Perrault, Observatoire, Paris, begun 1667. Grande Salle (Salle Cassini). (Photo: Philippe Sebert, Paris.) *left*

Figure 36. Claude Perrault, Observatoire, Paris, begun 1667. Stair. (Photo: Philippe Sebert, Paris.) *below*

objects, and those concerning the actions of clocks, barometers, and hydraulic devices. Before leaving, the Monarch examined a telescope almost 80 feet long. He judged the building to be "very beautiful" and "arranged in the best way."

The *Mercure* reported that three astronomers, including the Italian director, lived in the Observatoire, but there is nothing domestic about its architecture, which conveys the atmosphere of the rigorous think tank that it was designed to be. Four years later (1686), the building was proudly shown to Siamese ambassadors, and the *Mercure* again praised the stair, "as large as it is beautiful and bold. It is adorned with a rich iron balustrade [not the present one], and seems to hang in the air, being open [i.e., unsupported] in the center." The *Mercure* somewhat mysteriously concluded that Perrault's special knowledge of medicine (he was a physician by training) and mathematics had allowed him to incorporate things in the construction of the building "that all the other architects are not obliged to know." Those "things" to which the *Mercure* alludes may well have been the special expertise and experience of French masons and ironworkers (iron was used in the Louvre Colonnade; see Chap. 4) that Perrault especially appreciated and put to such remarkable use.

VERSAILLES – I (1661–1677)

If there is one building with which Louis XIV's name is inseparably linked, it is Versailles. Yet it is impossible to think of the palace itself without the environing garden within which it is set. The château and garden (and to some extent the town) form a gigantic whole, and the type of artistic thinking that brought them about, in which the constituent parts are transcended by a larger unity, has long been discerned as a basic quality of Baroque art, the label given by art historians to the artistic creations of the seventeenth and early eighteenth centuries. It would, however, be entirely mistaken to think that the palace, garden, and town were all conceived at one moment on some master planner's drawing board. Rather, the Sun King's Versailles developed, with many fits and starts, through the entire personal reign of the Monarch (over fifty years), although by the early 1690s, it had essentially reached its definitive form. It is universally considered to be the supreme architectural expression of absolute monarchy.

The evolution of Versailles is too complex to be gone into here, but a few essential facts about its development must be stated. In 1624, Louis XIV's father, Louis XIII, built a small hunting lodge near the village of Versailles, southwest of Paris. This was rebuilt in brick and stone in 1631–4 and accompanied by a modest garden. The building served as a *pied-à-terre* for royal hunting parties during the remainder of Louis XIII's reign (he died in 1643) and again during the 1650s, when the teenaged Louis XIV practiced hunting. With the initiation of his personal reign in 1661, the King unexpectedly began to develop Versailles in an ambitious manner, setting to work there the triumvirate that had created the splendors of Vaux-le-Vicomte (Chap. 3; Fig. 10): the architect Louis Le Vau (first architect of the King since 1654), the garden designer André Le Nôtre (in royal service since 1637 and the King's principal gardener since 1657), and the painter Charles Le Brun (called first painter of the King in documents from 1658 on), who also designed much of the garden sculpture. By 1668, a significant amount of work had been accomplished, as is revealed in a bird's-eye-view painting (Fig. 37): beginning in the lower part of the picture, we see three tree-lined converging roads (each with a wide central lane for coaches and narrower flanking ones for pedestrians) funneling into a large open space. These incipient avenues were to become the principal arteries of the new town of Versailles. The sides of the open space are defined by newly built cubelike pavilions for princes and courtiers, with the central feature at the rear being a preliminary oval courtyard introduced by obelisks (princely symbols), followed by sentry boxes and a grille with an opening leading to a further courtyard flanked by new buildings begun in 1662 for stables, kitchens, and servants' quarters. The pavilions and service buildings were in an old-fashioned brick-and-stone style to match the old château of Louis XIII, which appears at the rear of the rectangular courtyard. The new buildings were the work of Le Vau, who in 1662 or 1663 designed one of the first new features to appear in the park beyond the old garden – a Menagery for wild beasts laid out on a new, radiating plan, allowing the wedge-shaped animal pens to be observable from a central pavilion (Fig. 39). The fact that a zoo was one of the very first structures ordered by Louis XIV at Versailles is highly suggestive: menageries, frequently inhabited by ferocious animals, were often found at royal residences (there was one in the Tuileries garden in Paris). Besides providing amusement and sport (the beasts were sometimes allowed to fight each other), they were hoary symbols of the might of hunter–kings. The Versailles Menagery, however, was used to house rare creatures from distant climes rather than savage species, thus introducing the theme of the exotic, which we will encounter again at Versailles.

Another early and important architectural feature in the garden (again by Le Vau) was the Grotto of Tethys, a cubelike, flat-roofed structure that appears just behind the right-hand service building in Figure 37. Begun in 1664, the Grotto celebrated Louis in his *persona* of Apollo/Helios, and, like the Gallery of Apollo in the Louvre (begun 1663; Fig. 15), was one of the first works of architecture and decoration to do so. Lacking the naturalism of Italian grottoes, the one at Versailles was a regular architectural structure with three arched openings (vaguely reminiscent of the Arch of Constantine in Rome), closed by a grille with a pattern of bars radiating from the face of the sun god. The interior (Fig. 40), with walls and vaults decorated with colored rocks, contained three niches for spectacular marble sculptural groups of *Apollo Bathed by the Nymphs of Tethys* (by Girardon and Regnaudin, 1667–75) and the *Horses of Apollo Groomed and Fed by Tritons* (one group by Guérin, begun 1666, the other by the Marsy brothers, begun 1667). Inspired by the poetry of Ovid, the Grotto and its sculptures formed an allegory of Versailles as a place to which the Sun King retired after his strenuous exertions in governing the kingdom.

The painting of 1668 (Fig. 37) reveals the ongoing reshaping of the garden that had begun under Le Nôtre, probably in 1663. If we correlate this painting (in which we are looking due west) with a plan of perhaps the same year (Fig. 38), we see that the garden enclosing the château on three sides is divided into low open areas (*parterres*) with geometrical arrangements of greenery and water basins, and areas of massed trees *(bosquets),* which sometimes contain hidden features, such as fountains and sculpture. Nothing in this garden composition was to appear wild or in a natural state; all features proclaim the shaping forces of the human mind and hand and the victory of geometry over the irregular – the fundamental principles of the French formal garden.

By 1668, Le Nôtre had already established the two major axes that were to organize the garden and provide important vistas of varied sorts: the first running from east to west (that is, from the center of the garden façade of the château to the large water basin at the top of Figure 38 and beyond), the second laid out north–south and passing just in front of the garden façade. The painting shows the more important east–west axis already extended to a great distance. From the château, the axis passes between two grassy *parterres* to a small basin and steps overlooking a larger lower basin and *parterres* set in an expanded open space (sunlit in Fig. 37). Facing *bosquets* then define a tunnel of space leading to a farther basin (at the top of Fig. 38) and then a man-made canal with rows of trees extending out to the far distance and establishing a truly royal scale exceeding all earlier French gardens.

By 1672, the small basin nearest the château had been covered over, but the two others on the east–west axis had received important fountain sculptures that, like those in the Grotto, celebrated the myth of Apollo. The more distant lobed basin displays the *Apollo Fountain* (Fig. 41), showing the sun god in his horse-drawn chariot arising from the waters at break of day (by Tuby, 1668–70). Seen frontally and close up, the metal figures appear against the background of the canal, enhancing the illusion of emergence from the deep. When viewed from behind, the group funnels the gaze through a long corridor of space (the *Allée Royale*) to the *Latona Fountain* and the western façade of the palace. The *Latona Fountain* (by the Marsy brothers, 1668–70; Figs. 42 and 43) was originally at ground level; its present "wedding-cake" arrangement dates from 1687–9, and is an example of how frequently features at Versailles were modified or (as in the case of the Grotto of Tethys) completely destroyed (except for its sculptures). The central marble group of Latona and her divine twins, Apollo and Diana,

Figure 37. Pierre Patel, *View of Versailles*, 1668. Musée National du Château de Versailles. (Photo: Réunion des Musées Nationaux.)

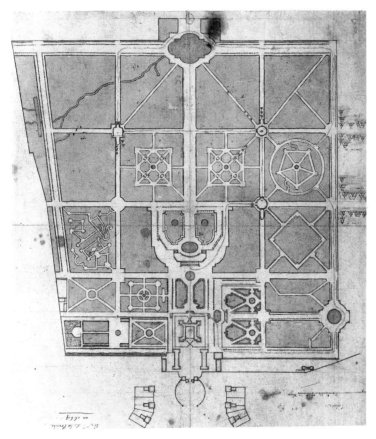

Figure 38. Plan of Versailles. Drawing by François de La Pointe, ca. 1668. Paris, Bibliothèque Nationale, Cabinet des Estampes. (Photo: Giraudon/Art Resource, New York.)

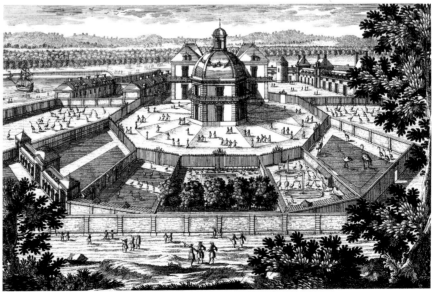

Figure 39. Louis Le Vau, Menagery, Versailles, begun 1662/3. Engraving by Pierre Aveline (1689). (Photo: Bibliothèque Nationale, Paris.)

Figure 40. Louis Le Vau, Grotto of Tethys, Versailles, begun 1664. Interior. Engraving by Jean Le Pautre (1676). (Photo: Bibliothèque Nationale, Paris.)

Figure 41. Jean-Baptiste Tuby, *Apollo Fountain*, Versailles, 1668–70. (Photo: Author.)

Figure 42. View of Latona Fountain (Marsy Brothers, 1668–70) and Allée Royale, Versailles. Engraving by Perelle. (Photo: Bibliothèque Nationale, Paris.)

Figure 43. View of Latona Fountain (Marsy Brothers, 1668–70; modified 1687–9) and Allée Royale, Versailles. (Photo: Author.)

appears surrounded by the wicked Lycian peasants, whom Jupiter is transforming into frogs at the behest of Latona. This somewhat unexpected theme may have been intended as an allegory of the civil wars of the Fronde (1648–52), with the central figures standing for Anne of Austria, Louis, and his brother Philippe, and the peasants, the *frondeurs*. In this interpretation, the fountain was a warning to those who would challenge the Crown.

In Figure 42, the length of the *Allée Royale* has been exaggerated by the engraver (cf. Fig. 43), but this depiction of the westerly vista extending virtually to the horizon seems like the perfect illustration of lines from a poem of ca. 1675 on the new Versailles:

> From the terrace one sees a very pleasing allée,
> Where royal grandeur is again displayed.
> It is in its extent a symbol or witness,
> Its length is so great, it reaches so far,
> That it appears without limit, and it is impossible
> To discover its imperceptible end by eyesight.
> The strongest eye cannot range everywhere
> Nor carry its glance from one end to the other.

These lines, written by a retired hydraulic engineer who had been in royal service, demonstrate that the vista was understood by contemporaries as a metaphor for royal grandeur and power. And that vista was accentuated by the subsequent extension of the Grand Canal (see Fig. 85).

Turning to the transverse north–south axis and to the area to the north of the château, Le Nôtre had to deal with a much shorter distance and land that sloped away from the palace. These features led him and Le Brun (who designed the sculpture and fountains) to create an axis meant to be explored on foot, where some features come unexpectedly into view, where monarchical allusions could be relaxed, and where a direct and intimate relationship between the work of art and the viewer could be established, all of this in contrast to the more formal east–west axis, exclusively concerned with Apollonian imagery, which can be grasped in all its grandeur from a fixed point.

In this northern part of the garden, Le Nôtre created a narrow, tunnellike vista defined by the high trees of the *bosquets* flanking the axis (Fig. 44, where the King proudly stands in the foreground with people of the court). We see that the axis first passed along the northern *parterre,* where complexly shaped compartments of grass are arranged around circular basins. These contain the *Fountains of the Crowns* (Fig. 45), in which sirens and tritons originally supported French royal crowns (by Tuby and Le Hongre, 1669–72; crowns replaced in 1685 by laurel wreaths, undoubtedly referring to Louis XIV). The axis leads to the *Fountain of the Pyramid* (by Girardon,

1669–71; Fig. 46), which, unlike the works of garden sculpture already discussed, was conceived as a purely decorative ornament, without allusion to the King. The fountain is of the candelabrum type, with a number of superposed, diminishing tiers, the whole set upon huge animal legs and base. The motifs of adult and child tritons, fish, and crayfish enliven the whole in a playful manner, and one of the tritons establishes direct contact with the spectator. At the same time, the vertical composition provides a focal point when viewed from below, where the land slopes more steeply away. A delicate water basin, the *Bath of Diana*, surprisingly comes into view to serve as a pedestal for the *Pyramid*. Its main bas-relief of bathing nymphs (by Girardon, 1669–70) continues the water theme that dominates this northern quarter of the garden. The flanking ramps lead on to the *Allée d'Eau* (begun 1668, with sculptures by several artists), two descending series of triads of children supporting marble basins. The decorative note and playful mood of the *Fountain of the Pyramid* are continued here with a new intimacy of scale. But at the bottom of the hill, in a clearing, Apollonian imagery reappears in the form of the *Dragon Fountain* (by the Marsy brothers, 1666–8; Fig. 47), for the dragon was understood to be the Python of mythology, slain by Apollo – the whole group referring again to the defeat of the Fronde.

Until 1679, the northern vista was halted by a wall behind the *Dragon Fountain* (for its prolongation by the *Neptune Basin,* see Chap. 10). The southerly part of the axis was developed near the château by a large flower *parterre* overlooking Le Vau's orangery built against a sudden drop of land, but the continuation and development of this axis into one of the most spectacular features of the garden must be left for a later phase of the story of Versailles (Chap. 10). Meanwhile, as these major axes were being developed, the *bosquets* were filled with very diverse features, including a labyrinth and fountains of ingenious variety.

The history of the château provides a clearer indication of the King's intentions for Versailles. Beginning in 1661, minor work was carried out on the exterior and interior of his father's brick-and-stone château, and in 1662, as we have already noted, two service wings were begun that defined a courtyard before the building (Figs. 37 and 38). This work, along with the expansion and adornment of the garden, suggested that Versailles was to remain a minor royal estate with a renovated garden suitable for outdoor festivities (the first of which was held in 1664). In 1668, however, the King made the momentous decision to greatly expand the size of the château so that it could serve as a suitable residence for himself and his family, and could be a setting for courtly functions, like the reception of dignitaries. The main problem was the old building: if it were preserved, the palace would seem out of date stylistically, but if it were razed, the King could be accused

Figure 44. Étienne Allegrain, *View of North Parterre, Versailles.* Grand Trianon, Versailles. (Photo: Réunion des Musées Nationaux.)

Figure 45. Jean-Baptiste Tuby and Étienne Le Hongre, *Fountain of the Crowns,* Versailles, 1669–72. (Photo: Author.)

Figure 46. François Girardon, *Fountain of the Pyramid*, Versailles, 1669–71. (Photo: Author.)

Figure 47. Marsy Brothers, *Dragon Fountain*, Versailles, 1666–8. (Photo: Author.)

of filial impiety. Le Vau in 1668 produced an ingenious design that retained Louis XIII's building (now called the Petit Château), but surrounded it on three sides with an entirely new construction, called the "Envelope." Work began in October of that year but was halted in 1669 when Louis XIV had a change of mind and ordered a competition for a palace without the older structure, which was to be torn down. Uncharacteristically reversing himself once again, the King later that year or early in 1670 returned to Le Vau's original Envelope scheme, which was then carried to completion in 1673/4.

Figure 49 is a plan of the main floor of the Envelope. If we compare it with Figure 48, we see how the Petit Château was incorporated into the new construction. The service buildings of the forecourt were enlarged and connected to the ends of the Envelope, and the entire design seen from the entrance side (Fig. 50) was in the old-fashioned brick-and-stone style of Louis XIII's Petit Château, visible at the rear of the successive courtyards. From the garden, however, the stylistically more progressive Envelope façades come into view (Figs. 51 and 52). They are entirely in stone without visible roofs, with a podiumlike, ground floor clearly distinguished from the *premier étage* on which the King lived, adorned with an Ionic order and terminated by an atticlike *deuxième étage* with stump pilasters. Statues were placed above the columnar projections of the main floor, and trophies and vases enliven the roof line. Le Vau's original design featured a western terrace (Fig. 51), reminiscent of Italian villas, and straight-topped windows at main floor level, but the terrace was later filled in and the windows arched to create the Galerie des Glaces (Chap. 10).

Unlike the Louvre, decisions about Versailles were taken in hand from the early 1660s on directly by Louis XIV, who continued to develop and expand the château and its garden against the wishes of Colbert, who wanted the King to finish the Louvre and principally reside there. Louis' compromise decision to retain the Petit Château was determined, as we have noted, by extra-artistic considerations, centering on the issue of filial piety, but his acceptance of Le Vau's solution to wed the old building to the new Envelope (Fig. 49) revealed an openness to unconventional planning. His approval of the Envelope elevation (Fig. 51) revealed that his taste was receptive to classicist style (as the Louvre Colonnade also demonstrated), albeit rooted, in this instance, in the vocabulary of the Italian High Renaissance. The Envelope was, to be sure, Le Vau's creation, but in its initial form it featured a colossal pilaster order embracing the upper two floors. Its modification into the executed elevation, which permitted a program of free-standing figural sculptures (depicting the months of the year, and the themes of flowers, fruits, and water) to be placed on projecting entablatures closer to the spectator, was probably arrived at after consultation with the Petite Académie (Chap. 3). Louis XIV's role in these decisions is veiled from

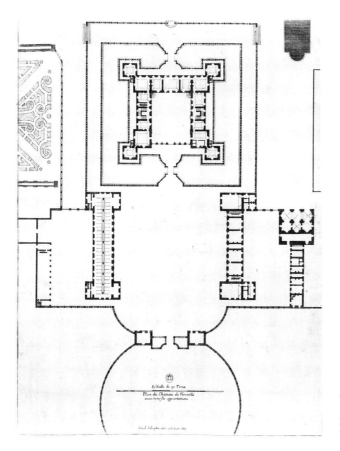

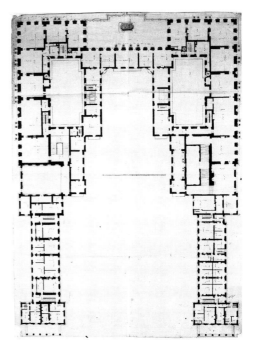

Figure 48. Petit Château, Versailles, 1631–4. Plan. Engraving by Israël Silvestre, 1667. (Photo: Bibliothèque Nationale, Paris.)

Figure 49. Château, Versailles. Plan of Main Floor with Envelope. Drawing, Stockholm, Nationalmuseum. (Photo: Statens Konstmuseer.)

our view, although we can at least observe that the importance of sculpture on the Envelope façades was consonant with its prominent use in the developing garden, of passionate concern to the King, who much later in his reign drew up itineraries for its visit (Chap. 10).

In retrospect, it is clear that a new royal scale for Versailles had first been established by 1668 in Le Nôtre's garden; the Envelope, designed in that year, recast the château into a grander edifice befitting the changed surroundings.

Now the interiors of the building were shaped as stage sets for its new ceremonial functions. The principal staircase, called the Ambassadors' Stair (destroyed; Fig. 53), was entered just before reaching the right wing of the Petit Château. The stair – designed after Le Vau's death in 1670 by his assistant and successor at Versailles, François d'Orbay – featured a central, moundlike podium of steps with two diverging flights parallel to the rear wall (a T-shaped stair rather than an imperial type; see Chap. 4), the whole contained within a single unified space (as in an imperial stair) with a low vault above and a large skylight. The profusion of marble-veneer walls with lavish gilding that characterizes the royal suites was introduced here. Le Brun designed illusionistic frescoes that seemed to spatially pierce walls and vault, and the marvels of this staircage were admired by the painted peoples of the world (including distant Asians, Africans, and native Americans) assembled in fictive loggias on the walls. The vault itself was frescoed (1674–80) with a very complex array of allegorical figures spelling out praise for Louis XIV, whose sculpted bust (Fig. 4) appeared above the

Figure 50. Château, Versailles, Entrance Side. (Photo: Author.)

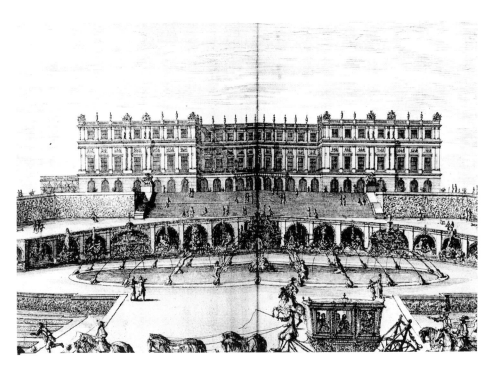

Figure 51. Louis Le Vau, West Façade of Envelope, Château, Versailles, begun 1668. Engraving by Israël Silvestre, detail (1674). (Photo: Bibliothèque Nationale, Paris.)

Figure 52. Louis Le Vau with Modifications by Jules Hardouin-Mansart, West Façade of Envelope, Château, Versailles. (Photo: Author.)

mound of steps. When ambassadors used this stair for official visits, the flights were impressively lined with soldiers.

The gilded doors at the tops of the flights led directly into the King's apartment, a suite of rooms within the northern wing of the Envelope, matched by an identical apartment for Queen Marie-Thérèse in the south range, both suites originally containing both ceremonial and functional rooms (Fig. 49). Rooms dating from the 1670s that have survived (Figs. 54 and 55) show the love for polychrome marble veneers in geometrical patterns, gilded woodwork, and heavy moldings, as in the Ambassadors' Stair. Unlike the Envelope exterior, the new interiors of Versailles revealed the King's persistent attraction to an Italianate Baroque vocabulary, reminiscent of the Louvre interiors of the 1650s in which he had grown up (Fig. 8).

Inside the château, images of the Sun King appear, and the painted ceilings display scenes from ancient history that were supposed to have been equalled by Louis XIV's deeds. Thus, the painting of *Jason and the Argonauts Debarking at Colchos* in the Salon of Diana was intended as an allusion to French colonization efforts. Each room was dedicated to one of the seven planets of Ptolemaic astronomy, with the central vault painting showing the planetary god or goddess in a chariot drawn by various animals, following an ancient tradition. In the original disposition of the rooms, that dedicated to the sun (Apollo) occupied the central position in each series of seven rooms, and the one on the King's side functioned as Louis XIV's throne room. In addition to these decorations, the royal apartments were hung with choice paintings from the King's collection (particularly from 1682 on), testimonials to the Monarch's taste as a collector.

In 1670, shortly before his death later that year, Le Vau designed an intriguing garden pavilion for Versailles called the Porcelain Trianon (the latter word deriving from the name of a small hamlet that formerly occupied the site) (Fig. 56). It was located at the end of the northern cross-arm of the canal (Fig. 85), corresponding to the placement of the Menagery (Fig. 39) at the end of the southern arm. The purpose of the building was to provide relaxation and meals for the King and his immediate suite. The main pavilion was not made of porcelain, of course, but of conventional materials, but its very French roof was adorned with ceramic decorations of vases, cupids, and birds (made in France and the Netherlands) and interiors that featured a blue-and-white color scheme. All of this was supposed to be in the "Chinese" style, despite the presence of pilasters, pediment, and a French roof. Yet, despite this naïveté, the Porcelain Trianon is significant in having been the first example of Far Eastern exoticism in Western architecture, the ancestor of many such "follies" set up in eighteenth-century European gardens. To enhance the exotic atmosphere, rare flowers were grown in the extensive garden.

It is unlikely that the idea for a Chinese pavilion originated with Le Vau. It is probably not coincidental that in 1670 a French translation of the Jesuit Athanasius Kircher's *China monumentis* of 1667 was published in Amsterdam with the simple title *La Chine*. This translation was dedicated to the French minister of war, the Marquis de Louvois (whom we shall encounter again in Chapter 9), and this may have brought the book to the attention of the French court, for the idea for a Porcelain Trianon arising from intellectual court circles is plausible, given the growing interest in China by the French during the seventeenth century. Like the exotic animals of the Menagery, the painted foreigners of the Ambassadors' Stair, and the art and curio collections housed in the château, the Porcelain Trianon contributed to the notion of Versailles as an amalgam of the rarities of the world.

The new town of Versailles, developed from the early 1670s on, is best studied in its plan (Fig. 85, bottom). The three wide converging avenues channeled incoming traffic to the parade ground (*Place d'Armes*) preceding the château, and the wedge-shaped areas between them became filled with important buildings, like the royal stables (Fig. 87). To the north and south of the avenues, the town was divided into rectangular blocks with small squares. Here were the private residential and commercial areas. The radiating avenues, however impressive as ceremonial conduits, had the negative effect of dividing the town into two quasi-independent quarters, where passage from one to the other had to traverse the considerable distance created by the avenues. Despite these drawbacks, the new town was a rare realization of a theoretical plan combining the traditional grid with the avenues of the ideal radial city of the Renaissance. (For documents that reveal the King's personal concern for roofing and paving in the town, see Chap. 3.)

Let us return to the question of why Louis XIV, certainly from 1668 on, was so intent on developing Versailles into an ambitious (and costly) residence. The French King had no lack of châteaux. Many, such as Fontaine-bleau and Saint-Germain-en-Laye, had been built by his Valois predecessors of the sixteenth century (particularly by Francis I; see Chap. 1), and most possessed extensive gardens. Then there was the Louvre-Tuileries complex in Paris with the Tuileries garden, which was under full development by 1668 (Chap. 4; Figs. 28 and 30). During the 1660s, Louis had not yet grown averse to Paris, even with its memories of the Fronde. Then why Versailles? It has been suggested that Versailles was developed so that the formerly turbulent French sword nobility (those of aristocratic blood who inherited their titles) could be domesticated into tame courtiers by being provided with a courtly center, a sort of stage set, where they would puff, strut, and fawn, all the while subtly controlled by the King and his officials.

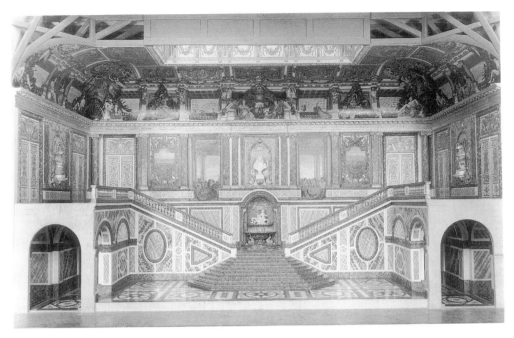

Figure 53. François d'Orbay, Ambassadors' Staircase, Versailles, 1674–80. Modern Model by Arquinet. Château of Versailles. (Photo: Réunion des Musées Nationaux.)

Figure 54. Château, Versailles, Salon of Venus, 1678–80. (Photo: Réunion des Musées Nationaux.)

Figure 55. Château, Versailles, Salon of Diana, 1670s. (Photo: Réunion des Musées Nationaux.)

Figure 56. Louis Le Vau, Porcelain Trianon, Versailles, 1670. Engraving by Pierre Aveline. (Photo: Bibliothèque Nationale, Paris.)

But the Louvre and Tuileries, Fontainebleau, Saint-Germain, and other royal châteaux were ready at hand for such purposes. Then why Versailles? Could it be, as has also been suggested, that the place had romantic meaning for the young King, for it was here that he frequently trysted with his first mistress, Louise de La Vallière. Yet this claim seems too tenuous in the light of the King's instinctive grasp of statecraft. The point, I believe, is that all of his substantial châteaux had some link to the pre-Bourbon past. That could be an advantage to a royal line anxious to affirm its legitimacy. (The first Bourbon king, Henry IV, had ascended the throne in 1589.) For Louis XIV, however, his father's modest hunting lodge – a purely Bourbon construction – could become the seed of a Bourbon architectural and artistic showcase, a new wonder of the modern world that would proclaim the glory of the Sun King and his royal house. Perhaps only Louis was able to glimpse this vision in 1668. Colbert, for most of the 1660s at least, wanted the Louvre to be Louis' principal residence, but ultimately failed. Funds for the new Louvre ran dry after 1680, and in 1682 Versailles was proclaimed the new royal capital (Chap. 10).

PARIS – I

In 1600 the city of Paris had a population estimated at 250,000 to 350,000; a hundred years later, it contained about half a million souls, making it the most populous and densest urban center in Europe. Important factors in this spectacular growth were a rural economic depression and political disruptions that began about 1630, driving large numbers of the rural poor and destitute to Paris in search of better conditions. Another contributing factor was the growth of government bureaucracy. Dynamic land speculation and development took place in Paris during the century, providing real estate not only for the aristocracy, but also for the newly rich robe nobility of merchants and financiers.

Compounding the growth in population was a transportation revolution caused by a sixteenth-century invention, the horse-drawn coach. Replacing the mule, the coach could carry several people much more rapidly. It was used for pleasure and for getting around town, and in 1662 appeared the "carrosse à cinq sous" (the five-penny coach) – the first omnibus, which continued in service until the end of the century. By 1700, it is estimated that there were about 20,000 coaches in Paris. If we add to this sum the other transportation modes also in use by the burgeoning population – litter chairs, wheeled chairs, carts, wagons, horses, and traditional mules – we can readily understand that major strains were being placed upon the urban fabric of the capital.

That urban fabric in 1661 – the year in which Louis XIV assumed personal rule of the kingdom – was still essentially medieval. Despite the urban renewal of Henry IV at the beginning of the century and work accomplished under Louis XIII, Paris in 1661 basically remained a warren of narrow, winding, unpaved streets. In addition to the mud and filth, there was crime, particularly at night. This is how the poet Paul Scarron described it:

Un amas confus de maisons,
Des crottes dans toutes les rues,
Ponts, églises, palais, prisons,
Boutiques bien ou mal pourvues,
. . .
Pages, laquais, voleurs de nuit,
Carrosses, chevaux, et grand bruit,
C'est là Paris: que vous en semble?

(A confused mass of houses,
Dirt in all the streets,
Bridges, churches, palaces, prisons,
Well or poorly provided shops,
. . .
Pages, lackeys, thieves of the night,
Coaches, horses, and loud noise,
That's Paris: how do you like it?)

Both Colbert and the King at the beginning of the 1660s perceived these conditions as intolerable in the capital of the realm. Although Louis was eventually to lose interest in Paris and physically abandon it for Versailles, during that first decade of his administration and during most of the 1670s, he was a sincere Parisian, interested in transforming Paris into a modern metropolis representative of the kingdom of France, the most powerful country in seventeenth-century Europe.

Beginning in 1662, a coherent plan of urban renewal and administration gradually took shape that lifted Paris out of its medieval past and into early modernity. The initiatives came not from the city government, but from the Crown. In 1662, Louis XIV began an annual subsidy for new street pavement and road repairs. In 1666 and 1667, a council was convened to survey the city and to make recommendations. Some of these were instituted in 1667: the position of lieutenant-general of police, concerned with public order, security, and public services; a "mud and lantern tax" applied to property owners to finance street cleaning and the placement of over 5,000 candle-lit lanterns that provided Paris with Europe's first system of public street illumination; and regulations controlling building height to admit more natural light into the streets (a maximum height of 15.6 meters was ordained for façades up to cornice level). Beginning in 1669, streets were widened and straightened, quais along the Seine (a major commercial artery) were enlarged or newly built, and the water-supply system was improved, with many new public fountains appearing from 1671 on (Fig. 58).

In addition to these important, utilitarian improvements, the King and Colbert began a program to give Paris a more ceremonial character, suited for its role as capital of France and the seat of its monarchy (Fig. 57). Two features were especially employed: the monumental avenue and the

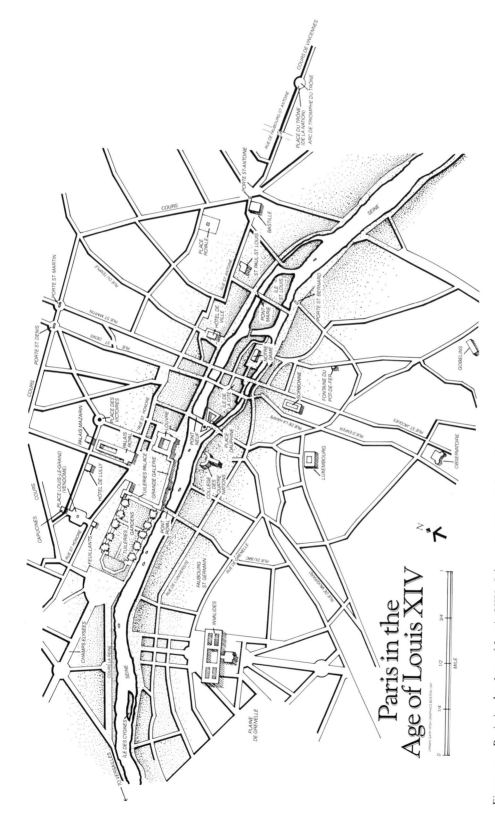

Paris in the Age of Louis XIV

Figure 57. Paris in the Age of Louis XIV. Schematic Map. Adapted from O. Ranum, *Paris in the Age of Absolutism*, New York, 1968. (Gary Irish Graphics, Boston.)

Figure 58. Fontaine du Pot-de-Fer, Paris, 1671. (Photo: Philippe Sebert, Paris.)

Figure 59. Claude Perrault, Arc de Triomphe du Trône, Paris, begun 1670. Engraving by Sébastien Le Clerc (1679). (Photo: Bibliothèque Nationale, Paris.)

Figure 60. Porte Saint-Antoine, Paris, 1585. Drawing, Bibliothèque Nationale, Paris, Cabinet des Estampes. (Photo: Bibliothèque Nationale, Paris.)

triumphal arch. Attention was first turned to the eastern approach to the city. Beginning in the 1660s, a straight, wide avenue was laid out between Vincennes to the east of Paris – the site of a royal château – and an open area closer to Paris, the Place du Trône (the present Place de la Nation). The latter was already connected to the Bastille at the eastern edge of the city (Right Bank) by the slightly irregular Rue du Faubourg Saint-Antoine. The avenue leading from Vincennes (the present Cours de Vincennes) was based (as were all the other avenues discussed in what follows) on the Cours-la-Reine (still in existence, although modified, along the river on the Right Bank), a precocious piece of urbanism ordered by Marie de Médicis in 1616. This nearly one-mile-long stretch outside the city walls consisted of a very wide central lane, suitable for coaches, flanked by a narrow path on each side for pedestrians, with rows of trees serving as dividers. The new avenue from Vincennes was laid out in the same manner. (This type of avenue had also been introduced at Versailles by 1668; see Chap. 6 and Fig. 37.) But whereas the Cours-la-Reine was intended for recreation (parading of coaches) and ended not far from the city, the new avenue was intended as a stately and monumental approach to Paris, to be heightened by a huge triumphal arch to be erected on the site of the Place du Trône.

For the design of this arch, a competition was held during 1668–9 among Le Vau, Le Brun, and Perrault, and it was the Perrault's proposal that won the day (Fig. 59). A temporary full-scale mockup of Perrault's Arc de Triomphe du Trône, as it was called, was quickly erected at the *place* in 1669–70; in the latter year, foundations were laid for the permanent structure, but the arch never rose more than a few feet above ground for lack of sustained funding. Nevertheless, Perrault's design is an important statement of the new aesthetic of the Sun King's buildings.

Triumphal arches, consciously based on ancient Roman examples, had been erected in Paris during the sixteenth century, but almost always as temporary structures for the entrance ceremonies of rulers. In 1585, one of these arches, known as the Porte Saint-Antoine, was rebuilt in durable materials as the city's first permanent arch (Fig. 60). It was still standing in its original form when Perrault won the competition in 1669, and a comparison of it with his Arc de Triomphe du Trône makes clear the monumental and classicist qualities of the new architecture. The Porte Saint-Antoine resembles the upper half of a contemporary church façade with a central archway borrowed from domestic architecture inserted into it. The main entablature is almost obliterated by an inscription plaque and sculpted ships (the symbols of Paris), thus weakening the architectonic expression. Other sculptures and obelisks enliven the silhouette, again leading the eye away from the purely architectural features, such as walls, piers, and pediment. Nothing about the Porte is reminiscent of ancient Rome. By contrast, the Arc de Triomphe du Trône clearly emulates triple-arched Roman examples, such as the Arch of Constantine. Although Perrault's arch is loaded with sculpture-in-the-round and sculpted reliefs, the decoration does not interrupt or project away from the purely architectonic forms, except for the culminating equestrian statue of the King at the summit. The scale is immense, and had it been built, this triumphal arch would have been the largest in the world.

In the same year that work was started on Perrault's arch (1670), the King and Colbert moved aggressively ahead with their urban program for Paris. The fortifications around the northern periphery, built under Louis XIII between 1643 and 1647, began to be razed, the moat was filled in, and new, broad avenues, identical to the Cours-la-Reine and the road from Vincennes, started to be built on top of the razed fortification wall. The destruction of the old ramparts signaled that the capital was secure from foreign and domestic foes. Work began at the Porte Saint-Antoine, on the eastern side of the city, and progressed counterclockwise in a great arc, so that by about 1700, the new Cours (Fig. 61), as it was called, reached the

Figure 61. Cours, Paris, begun 1670. Engraving. (Photo: Bibliothèque Nationale, Paris.)

location of the present Place de la Concorde. The Cours, like the Cours-la-Reine, was used for recreation; commercial traffic was barred in 1679, diverted to a lower road parallel to the Cours. A matching Cours for the Left Bank was intended by Louis XIV and Colbert, but little progress was made during the King's reign. (The present Grands Boulevards of the Right Bank follow the path of the seventeenth-century Cours.)

In 1671, the mathematician François Blondel, a member of the Royal Academy of Sciences, was officially appointed controller-general of Parisian works by the Crown. (In the same year, he was also named director of the newly founded Royal Academy of Architecture; Chap. 3.) In the previous year, Blondel had rebuilt the Porte Saint-Bernard, and he continued to focus his attention, after being named to the new post, on the old gateways on the periphery of the city. In 1671, he remodeled the Porte Saint-Antoine and designed the extant Porte Saint-Denis (built 1671–2, sculptural decoration finished in 1676; Fig. 62). Although not as overtly classicistic as Perrault's arch, the Porte Saint-Denis likewise subordinates sculptural decoration to the architectonic lines of the structure. The sculpture celebrates France's victories in the contemporary Dutch War. Massive piers flanking the single great archway enclose high relief obelisks – traditional symbols of princely power – capped with orbs bearing the royal French crown and fleurs-de-lis. Military trophies hung from laurel trees adorn the obelisks. On the side of the arch facing the city, at the bases of the obelisks, sit personifications of

Figure 62. François Blondel, Porte Saint-Denis, Paris, 1671–6. (Photo: Author.)

Figure 63. Pierre Bullet, Porte Saint-Martin, Paris, 1674–7. (Photo: Author.)

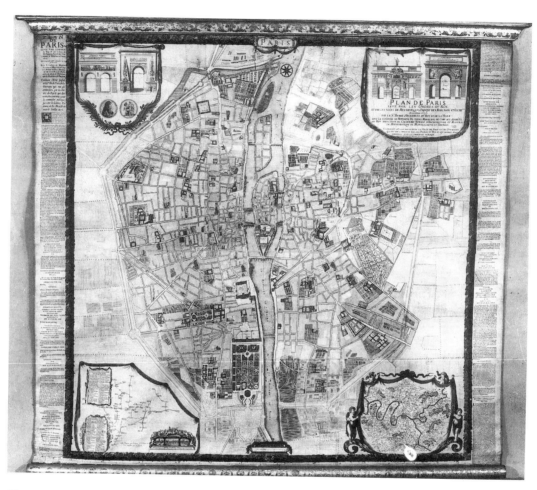

Figure 64. François Blondel and Pierre Bullet, Map of Paris, 1675–6. (Photo: Giraudon/Art Resource, New York.)

Figure 65. Jacques IV Gabriel, Pont-Royal, Paris, 1685–9. Engraving by Liéven Cruyl. (Photo: Giraudon/Art Resource, New York.)

hapless Holland (left) and the river Rhine (right), which Louis and his army crossed in a bold campaign in 1672. The river crossing is depicted as a realistic narrative in the rectangular relief above the archway, and Victory figures in the spandrels with trumpet and wreath add to the triumphal note. The exterior face displays crouching lions (symbols of the Netherlands) at the bases of the obelisks, with reliefs of the capture of Maestricht by the French in 1673. The pedestals below the obelisks, with military motifs in low relief, were consciously patterned after the pedestal of Trajan's Column in Rome, and Blondel complained in his *Cours d'architecture* (1683) that he was forced by the city of Paris to open passages for pedestrians in these pedestals, which he felt visually weakened the effect.

The Porte Saint-Denis provided a monumental entranceway from the north into the metropolis; standing not far to the east is the extant companion arch, the Porte Saint-Martin, the work of Blondel's pupil Pierre Bullet (1674–5, sculptural decoration finished in 1677; Fig. 63). Both arches, initiated by the Crown, were paid for by the city. The more horizontal proportions of Bullet's arch and its high attic for the inscription in honor of the King recall ancient Roman prototypes, even though the orders are lacking in favor of vermiculated rustication, which lends a somewhat fortified quality to the arch. Again, the sculpture does not disturb the architectural lines. The reliefs on the city side (shown in Fig. 63) are allegories of two triumphs of the Dutch War: the rupture of the Triple Alliance (left: the King in the guise of Hercules, crowned by a Victory, stands over the body of Gereon) and the capture of Besançon (right: a personification of the defeated city kneels at Louis' feet, while a Victory hovers above blowing a trumpet). The exterior side of the arch depicts Mars repelling an eagle (an allegory of the defeat of Germany) and the capture of Limbourg (1675).

Blondel and Bullet collaborated in 1675 in drawing up a map of Paris that, after having been approved by Louis XIV, was published the next year (Fig. 64). An innovation in the history of cartography, this city map depicted not only existing features, but also projected ones, including the complete system of avenues for both Banks and newly built and/or improved quais and streets. A small map-within-the-map depicts the water-pipe system for the city and its *faubourgs*, with indications of the forty fountains, sixteen of which were new (Fig. 58). Blondel and Bullet, however, did not attempt to propose radically new traffic patterns within Paris, nor did they envision the creation of new squares, a phenomenon that began in the 1680s (Chap. 12).

One additional urban improvement belonging to that decade, but that I mention here, is a new stone bridge, the Pont-Royal (1685–9), which the Crown paid for as a replacement of the old wooden Pont-Rouge that had burned in 1684. This extant bridge (Fig. 65) was built farther to the west than its predecessor in order to be in alignment with the Pavillon de Flore (at the juncture of the Tuileries Palace and the Grande Galerie) and the Rue du Bac on the Left Bank. Like the older Pont-Neuf, it was built without houses, providing splendid views over the river to those traveling upon it. The Pont-Royal was designed by Jacques IV Gabriel and was executed under the Flemish Dominican priest François Romain, a technical expert.

In 1676, Louis XIV imported a number of swans and placed them on an island in the Seine at the west end of the city. (The island, then called the Ile Maquerelle, became known as the Ile des Cygnes [Island of Swans], which in 1773 was attached to the Left Bank and survives as the Port du Gros-Caillou.) Special legislation was passed to protect the birds, who could be seen up and down the river and especially by people on the road to Versailles or on the Cours-la-Reine. The King surely thought of the swans as graceful adornments to Paris, but he also must have known that the bird was associated with Apollo (swans appear in the Dragon Fountain at Versailles [Fig. 47], where they refer to Louis). With one stroke, the Sun King embellished the city and multiplied reminders of his favorite *persona* for all to see.

A PALACE FOR A MISTRESS
The Chateau of Clagny and the Rise of Jules Hardouin-Mansart

In 1660, Louis XIV, then twenty-two, married the Spanish Infanta, Maria-Teresa, the daughter of Philip IV of Spain. Thus were the houses of Bourbon and Hapsburg linked in a union based principally on power politics rather than on love. There is no indication that Marie-Thérèse (as she was called in France) ever captivated the French king; indeed, he seems to have been bored for the most part with his pious and dull foreign queen, whose vacuous face has been preserved by the brushes of Velázquez and French court portraitists.

Early in his marriage, Louis took a mistress, a lovely unmarried girl at court named Louise-Françoise de La Baume Le Blanc, later (1667) the Duchesse de La Vallière. There was no secrecy about the matter: French kings of the house of Valois had openly taken mistresses since Charles VII in the midfifteenth century, and Louis' grandfather, Henry IV, had adopted the practice for the Bourbon line. The role of royal mistress had acquired a semiofficial status in France well before the Sun King's time. (Louis even wrote openly about La Vallière in his *Mémoires for the Instruction of the Dauphin.*)

La Vallière was to bear the King six children, but in 1666 or 1667, when she was still the official mistress, Louis' roving eye fell upon a married aristocratic woman at court, Françoise-Athénaïs de Rochechouart de Mortemart, Duchesse de Montespan. Educated, witty, and beautiful, she was descended from an ancient French aristocratic family. Thus began a double adultery. Her aggrieved husband, the Marquis de Montespan, had the audacity to openly protest the Sun King's sexual imperialism. One fine day, he drove up to the royal Château of Saint-Germain in a coach draped in black (in mourning for his wife), decorated with deer antlers (the cuckold's emblem). For this bizarre behavior, the Marquis was exiled to his estate in the south of France. But the King continued to receive implicit criticism of

Figure 66. Antoine Le Pautre, Design for the Château of Clagny. Garden Façade. Drawing, 1674. Nationalmuseum, Stockholm. (Photo: Statens Konstmuseer.)

his behavior from another quarter: The Archbishop of Sens pointedly punished a woman for living in sin, and published old Church laws against adultery in his dioceses, which included Fontainebleau, site of a much-frequented royal château.

In the spring of 1674, when Louis' liaison with Madame de Montespan was at its height, the Parlement of Paris at last legally separated the Montespans, and the King immediately commissioned a house for his mistress and her royal bastards (she eventually bore him eight) at Clagny, a suburb of Versailles. The awarding of châteaux to royal mistresses had a long tradition in France, beginning with Charles VII, who gave Agnès Sorel Beauté-sur-Marne; other famous instances include Diane de Poitiers' Anet, paid for by Henry II, and Montceaux-en-Brie, given to Gabrielle d'Estrées by Henry IV.

The post of first architect was still vacant since the death of Louis Le Vau in 1670, so for Clagny, Louis turned to Antoine Le Pautre, his brother's architect, who was busy at the time with Philippe's château at Saint-Cloud. Le Pautre designed Clagny in April or May, 1674, the plans were approved by the King (they were sent to him while he was on a military campaign in Franche-Comté) and by his mistress, and construction began that year.

Drawings preserved in Stockholm (one is shown in Fig. 66) reveal that Le Pautre had designed a *maison de plaisance* of exceptional lightness of feeling and restraint. Evidently consisting of a *corps-de-logis* and wings arranged in a U-shaped plan, the small château featured a main floor at ground level surmounted by a mezzanine story, the whole forming a long, low silhouette. A domed central pavilion harbored a two-story salon. On the exterior, simply framed windows and relief panels were quietly distributed against the blank walls, with quoining strips providing the only textural contrast. On the interior appeared delicate, thin moldings and swags. The entire design was probably meant to exude an air of femininity, suitable to its main occupant.

As the building was rising, or perhaps when it was finished, Madame de Montespan changed her mind and condemned the château as too small and unsuited to her rank, fit only for an opera singer ("une fille d'opéra"). Another of Le Pautre's drawings, with different proposals for columns or pilasters to monumentalize the courtyard walls, may represent the architect's frantic attempt to revise his design and please his difficult patron. If so, his labors were in vain, for Le Pautre was dismissed, the building was torn down, and a new architect was brought upon the scene, with momentous consequences for the history of French architecture.

That architect was Jules Hardouin-Mansart, and early sources tell us that it was Le Nôtre who recommended him to the King and his mistress at the time of the crisis over Le Pautre's château. The year was 1675. Hardouin-Mansart quickly devised a new design that was begun that year. Before we turn to this project, however, it is appropriate to review the early years of this figure who was to go on to a fabulously successful and long career as the King's first architect.

Jules Hardouin, as he was originally named, was born in 1646, a great-nephew of the renowned architect François Mansart. In 1660, after the death of his father, a painter, the fourteen-year-old Jules was apprenticed to his great-uncle to learn the art of architecture. During the 1660s, Jules Hardouin obtained his first professional experiences at some of his uncle's buildings in and around Paris. Upon Mansart's demise in 1666, Jules coupled the former's name to his: Hardouin-Mansart. In its basic outline, the younger Mansart's early biography was typical of French architects of his day (including Le Vau): birth into a family with the father or a relative an architect, artist or artisan, or in the building trades; lack of a good general education; apprenticeship beginning in one's teens.

After his uncle's death, Jules launched upon an independent career, working at many sites in the north and south of France. Beginning in 1669, he received commissions for small residences in the new areas of the town of Versailles. In 1673, Colbert dispatched him to the Midi to assist in the creation of the Canal des Deux-Mers, apparently in an engineering capacity, and he visited the Pont du Gard and the Roman antiquities at Nîmes. Also, in 1673, he designed the Hôtel de Ville in Arles, with an astonishing vault. Colbert may have employed him in a minor way about 1674–5 at his Château of Sceaux after his return to the north. Perhaps about the same time, the young architect also came to the notice of the secretary of war, the Marquis de Louvois (Mansart's later patron at the Invalides; Chap. 9), who, according to an early, anonymous biographer, ordered him to design a public building in Tournai, a Flemish city that had been captured by the French in 1667. Then, in 1675, came the breakthrough: two royal commis-

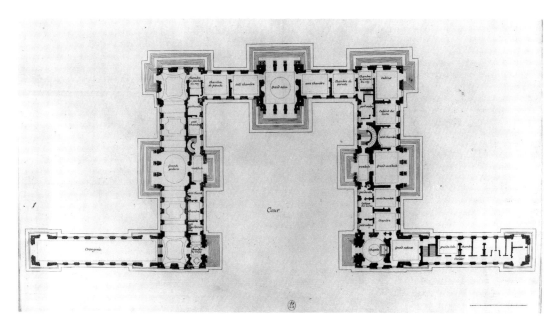

Figure 67. Jules Hardouin-Mansart, Château of Clagny, begun 1675. Plan of Ground Floor. Engraving by Michel Hardouin (1678). (Photo: Bibliothèque Nationale, Paris.)

sions, the Château du Val, a small, one-story hunting pavilion in the forest of Saint-Germain-en-Laye for the King, and the Château of Clagny. (Additionally, Hardouin-Mansart became a member of the Royal Academy of Architecture in the same year.)

Mansart's Clagny was built from 1675 to 1682, years that encompassed Montespan's fall from royal favor and her replacement by Madame de Maintenon, whom the King secretly married in 1684, one year after the death of Queen Marie-Thérèse. Although the château was eventually totally demolished in 1769, an abundance of drawings and prints gives us a good idea of the building (Figs. 67–9). It was placed at one end of a large natural pond, with its entrance façade facing east (like the Château of Versailles), so that from its western windows and garden could be seen the pond and a good deal of Versailles. Like its predecessor, Clagny II was built in a traditional U-plan, with a domed *corps-de-logis* at the rear of the court and two wings at right angles. There was now a full upper floor covered with *mansarde* roofs. The building was supplemented by two low wings that extended perpendicularly from the ends of the main wings. These low wings (Fig. 67) contained an orangery (left) and a kitchen and rooms for servants (right), functional spaces that were usually built separately from the main château itself. By attaching these units to the ends of the main wings and designing them only one floor high without visible roofs (Fig. 68), Mansart showed a liking early in his career for a sprawling plan that emphasized horizontality and earth-hugging forms – features that were to reappear in later domestic works, particularly the Trianon de Marbre at Versailles (Chaps. 10 and 14).

The main pavilion at the rear of the court (Fig. 68) consisted of a two-story columnar portico with pediment, surmounted by a four-sided dome decorated in lead with a radiant Apollo's head. This monumental unit – far more imposing than Le Pautre's columnless pavilion (Fig. 66) – led into a domed, two-story salon, articulated with pilasters and niches for sculpture. The salon communicated directly with the garden and with apartments extending from the *corps-de-logis* and into the two wings (Fig. 67). The other major display piece of the interior was a long gallery placed in the left

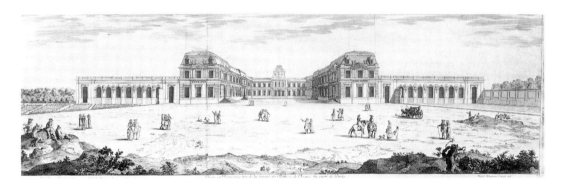

Figure 68. Jules Hardouin-Mansart, Château of Clagny, begun 1675. Entrance Side. Engraving by Michel Hardouin (1678). (Photo: Bibliothèque Nationale, Paris.)

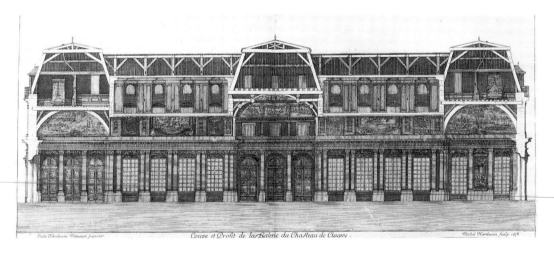

Figure 69. Jules Hardouin-Mansart, Château of Clagny, begun 1675. Section of Gallery Wing. Engraving by Michel Hardouin (1678). (Photo: Bibliothèque Nationale, Paris.)

Figure 70. Anonymous French Painter, *Madame de Monte-span in the Château of Clagny,* 1670s. Uffizi, Florence. (Photo: Alinari/Art Resource, New York.)

wing (Figs. 67 and 69). The gallery was flanked at each end by square, domed salons (prefiguring the Salon de la Guerre and Salon de la Paix at Versailles; Chap. 10), and its three central bays were similarly covered by a separate cupola, higher than the barrel vaults that ran above the main bays of the gallery. These bays interrupted the continuity of the room, but in this way, Mansart made the central part of the gallery serve the additional function of a separate salon linking an oblong vestibule on the court side with the garden. The barrel vault was filled with a number of framed fields that were to be painted and accompanied by stucco sculpture, in the formula derived from the Gallery of Apollo in the Louvre (Fig. 15). The main stair, in the right wing (Fig. 67), featured curving flights and a structure that the *Mercure galant* in 1686 described as "extraordinaire" (we lack details of its exact form). Clearly, the architecture and decorations of the building were intended to rival the best royal work.

The garden, by Le Nôtre, was in his traditional style, with *parterres* and *bosquets* of varied geometrical shapes set within a rectangular grid of axes. A *parterre de broderie* was set before the garden façade of the main block, and paths flanking it led directly to a semicircle of land projecting into the pond, whence could be viewed the splendid panorama of Versailles.

The history of Clagny makes clear that the real patron was Madame de Montespan, whose every whim was granted by her royal lover. An anonymous painting (Fig. 70), perhaps from the late 1670s, shows the imperious beauty reclining on a day bed within what purports to be her château. Her role as a sexual object is unambiguous; what is at question is the depiction of the gallery in the background. Comparisons with the engraved views (Fig. 69) reveal that the painted view is a fantasy, giving the room an inflated scale (note particularly the higher, semicircular vault). Perhaps the painted architecture represents a daydream of La Montespan, never satisfied with even a King's munificence.

THE INVALIDES

War veterans – particularly the disabled and indigent – had constituted a social problem in France ever since the Hundred Years War. They were difficult to reintegrate into society after hostilities, and were placed in religious houses as lay members or oblates. This custom proved ineffectual and the veterans tended to form an urban rabble or a rural band of brigands (whenever they were periodically expelled from Paris) that was perceived with disdain and fear. Homes for them were proposed and sometimes founded beginning with the reign of Henry IV (1589–1610), but without real success. In 1670, two years after the end of Louis XIV's first foreign war – the War of Devolution (1667–8) – the King resolved to create an institution on a new scale that would flourish and act as an inducement to potential military recruits. The Hôtel des Invalides received veterans and disabled soldiers who lived a semimonastic life within its confines, spending their time doing handicrafts (including knitting and manuscript illumination) and attending church twice daily. The Hôtel was intended to house a self-sufficient community of several thousand, and included living quarters, refectories (Fig. 74), a vegetable garden, brewery, cemetery and other features.

The King entrusted the enterprise not to Colbert, his superintendent of the King's buildings, but to his secretary of war, the Marquis de Louvois (technically, the associate secretary who succeeded his father, Michel Le Tellier, who held the post until his death in 1677). It is uncertain whether the King in 1670 was already thinking of the young Louvois as Colbert's future successor as superintendent. But the Invalides turned out to be a perfect training ground for this position, for Louvois later succeeded Colbert in this capacity in 1683 upon the latter's death.

A suburban, undeveloped location was chosen for the Hôtel on the Plaine de Grenelle, to the west of the Faubourg Saint-Germain on the Left Bank of

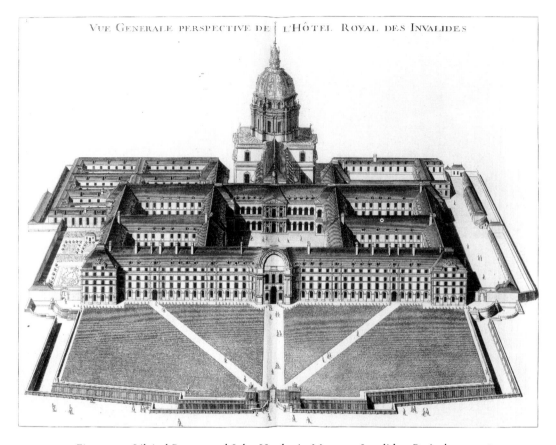

VUE GÉNÉRALE PERSPECTIVE DE L'HÔTEL ROYAL DES INVALIDES

Figure 71. Libéral Bruant and Jules Hardouin-Mansart, Invalides, Paris, begun 1671. Bird's-Eye View. Engraving from J. F. Félibien, *Description de l'église royale des Invalides,* Paris, 1706. (Photo: Houghton Library, Harvard University.)

Paris. Such locations were traditional for hospitals, and one of the functions of the new establishment was to provide care for the war-wounded. A guidebook to Paris of 1685 states that a competition had been held in 1670 that was won by Libéral Bruant, a minor architect. The following year, Bruant signed a contract and construction began, with Louis XIV laying the first stone. By late 1674, the fabric had progressed to a point that allowed the first veterans to be installed.

The huge building (Fig. 71) was organized as a grid, with a main central courtyard flanked by two smaller ones on each side and additional courts to the rear (south). The enormous northern entrance façade is articulated, in typical French fashion, by central and end pavilions, which project forward. The welcoming entrance arch of the central pavilion rests on piers adorned with pairs of Ionic pilasters. This is the sole appearance of the orders on the exterior; the remainder of the four-story façade is horizontally divided by stringcourses and an entablature, with vertical quoining strips occasionally

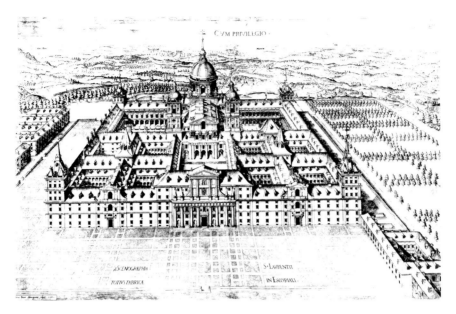

Figure 72. Juan Bautista de Toledo and Juan de Herrera, El Escorial, 1563–82. Bird's-Eye View. Engraving from J. de Herrera, *Sumario y breve declaracion de los diseños y estampas de la farbrica de San Lorencio el Real del Escurial,* Madrid, 1589. (Photo: Harvard College Library.)

Figure 73. Libéral Bruant, Hôtel des Invalides, Paris, begun 1671. Courtyard. (Photo: Author.)

relieving the monotony. But this austere, barrackslike architecture is unexpectedly relieved by rich and humorous touches: the continuous frieze of trophies on the entrance arch, culminating in a radiant Apollo's head at the summit, the luxuriant display of trophies above the dormers of the end pavilions, and, especially, the lighthearted framing of the dormers with suits of armor, some with faces beneath the helmets. (The equestrian relief of Louis XIV within the entrance arch dates from the 1730s, as did the seated statues on pedestals, now replaced by modern copies.)

Despite these details, the dominant imagery recalls both military barracks and monastery, and this theme is further developed in the main courtyard (Fig. 73), with its austere ranges of arches on piers, defining the surrounding two-story porticoes, slightly relieved by pedimented pavilions at the centers of each range. Once again, the severe atmosphere is lightened, this time by frisky, rearing horses above the projecting corners of the court and by the trophies framing the dormer windows.

As early as 1673, Louvois had become dissatisfied with Bruant, whom he perceived as slow and possibly dishonest. Although the Hôtel was nearing completion, it still lacked an essential element – a chapel. This was to be placed on the central axis to the south of the main court, the entire complex thereby recalling the Escorial in Spain, Bruant's probable model (Fig. 72). During 1675, a chapel project was devised by Bruant and submitted in January 1676 for a critique to François Blondel, the director of the recently founded Royal Academy of Architecture. Blondel's negative criticism enables us to grasp some essential details of the chapel. It was a basilican church with a transept, nave, and side aisles, the nave covered with a barrel vault with lunettes, the side aisles supporting galleries above. Although Blondel was critical of many features of this proposal, it is evident that Louvois did not dismiss it out of hand. Two months later, in March 1676, we find Louvois in contact with a young architect, Jules Hardouin-Mansart, who had entered royal service the preceding year for the King and his mistress, Madame de Montespan, and whom Louvois may have already used to design a building in Tournai (see Chap. 8). At the Invalides, Hardouin-Mansart replaced Bruant for the chapel project, although the latter remained as architect of the Hôtel until some remaining work there was finished in 1676.

From March 1676 on, Hardouin-Mansart proceeded rapidly toward a solution of the chapel problem. Surprisingly, he designed two linked churches: a basilica (the Soldiers' Church) attached to a central-plan domed edifice (the Dôme) (Fig. 75). The Dôme was worked out as early as March–April 1676, then refined, and a model was made. This was shown to Louis XIV in February 1677, and contracts followed that same month (for the foundations) and in December (for the superstructure); construction started immediately thereafter. As for the Soldiers' Church, it was evidently designed between March and November 1676; a contract was signed in the latter month, and the church started to rise in 1677 and was roofed that same year.

The Soldiers' Church, designed by Mansart in 1676, was built from 1677 to 1679. Surprisingly, it would seem to closely resemble the project by Bruant that Blondel had criticized in January 1676. The realized structure (Figs. 75 and 76) has all the features of the earlier proposal, except that the aisles are narrower and there is no transept. Also lacking is the crossing covered by a depressed vault on four piers that is specified in Blondel's critique. Otherwise, what we see today is a variant on Bruant's scheme, even with the retention of specific features like the galleries with depressed arches that the academician had specifically condemned. It is evident that Louvois had not been entirely dissuaded by Blondel's opinions, and instructed Mansart to retain Bruant's project, but with variations.

The pedimented pavilion in the center of the south range of the main court (Fig. 73) is adorned with full, superposed orders with paired columns (Composite over Ionic) to form shallow porches in two stories – the façade of the Soldiers' Church, designed by Bruant. This leads into a portico, then a severe rectangular vestibule, followed by the chapel (Fig. 76). The visitor's eyes are immediately struck by the colorful display of captured flags lining the nave, a continuation of the custom from the time of Louis XIV of hanging enemy standards from the main vault. We should imagine the Soldiers' Church filled with the King's crusty old veterans and *mutilés,* with the captured enemy flags forming a canopy of martial glory above them.

The long nave is covered by a barrel vault with lunettes and flanked by a vaulted aisle on each side with a vaulted gallery above. The nave is articulated by nine bays formed by arches on piers, with colossal Corinthian pilasters applied to the faces of the piers and supporting a full, continuous entablature above. Whereas the ground-floor arches are semicircular, the arches of the galleries above are depressed. This entire nave elevation with its vault of revealed stereotomy and large clerestory windows is directly quoted from the principal Jesuit church in Paris, Saint-Paul-Saint-Louis (Fig. 77), the differences being in the treatment of the frieze of the main entablature (unornamented at the Invalides, acanthus scroll at the Jesuits) and the balustrade at gallery level (ovals and rectangles at the Invalides, balusters at the Jesuits). The Jesuit church, begun in 1627, was originally dedicated only to Saint Louis (King Louis IX of France). It was completed in 1641, when Louis XIII declared it to be a royal foundation. The undisguised dependence of the interior of the Soldiers' Church on the older building may be due to their common dedication (the Soldiers' Church was also dedicated to Saint Louis) and to the fact that both were royal buildings. Bruant certainly

Figure 74. Libéral Bruant, Hôtel des Invalides, Paris, begun 1671. Refectory. Engraving by Jean Le Pautre. (Photo: Bibliothèque Nationale, Paris.)

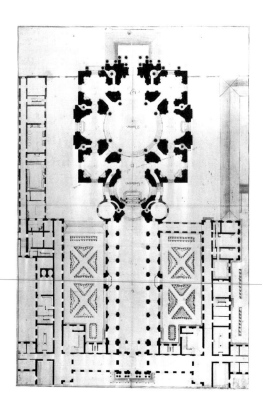

Figure 75. Jules Hardouin-Mansart, Plan of Soldiers' Church and Dôme, Invalides, Paris, begun 1677. Drawing, Bibliothèque Nationale, Paris, Cabinet des Estampes. (Photo: Bibliothèque Nationale, Paris.)

Figure 76. Jules Hardouin-Mansart, Soldiers' Church, Invalides, Paris, begun 1677. Interior. (Photo: Author.)

knew it well, for the Jesuit Maison Professe, as it was called, was Bruant's parish church.

The contract of November 1676 for the church refers to it as a "choeur d'église" (church choir). This is puzzling until we consider Mansart's second church, the Dôme of the Invalides, also designed in 1676 (with later modifications). Looking at the plan of the two linked buildings (Fig. 75), we see that the main entrance to the Dôme, for the general public, is marked by a large outdoor stair to the south; the Soldiers' Church then can be understood as forming a private retrochoir housing a special congregation (the veterans) that can view a common altar set up in the oval apse of the Dôme. In this way, the soldiers and the public are kept apart in distinct architectural environments, yet can share in the same divine service.

The Dôme of the Invalides, however, is a surprisingly large, monumental structure (Figs. 78 and 79). If we recall that its location on the Plaine de Grenelle was suburban and countrified in the seventeenth century, we may well wonder why such an elaborate building was erected to serve the relatively few inhabitants of the area. Its grandeur and size seem inappropriate for a parish church. But the Dôme was not built for parishoners. Dedicated

Figure 77. François Derand, Saint-Paul-Saint-Louis, Paris, begun 1627. Interior. (Photo: Author.)

to the Holy Trinity, but named after Saint Louis (like the Soldiers' Church), the Dôme was only opened upon the occasion of royal visits and seems to have been originally conceived as a sacred building commemorating the military glory of Louis XIV and his armies. The key to this interpretation is provided by a detailed account of the first intended decoration of the main cupola by the artist Charles de La Fosse, who painted a model of the dome before February 1677 (lost). La Fosse described a heavenly scene in which the Holy Trinity blesses the arms of Louis XIV, presented by four angels, as Saints Louis and Charlemagne pray to the Trinity for the King's weapons to conquer all enemies. The military theme was further emphasized in the painting by groups of Old Testament warriors, the sainted soldiers of the Church Militant, and the female heroines Joan of Arc, Judith, Deborah, and Jael. The spectacle included personifications of the Netherlands, Flanders, and Franche-Comté, reminders that in 1676 France was in the midst of Louis XIV's second major foreign war, the Dutch War (1672–8), and that French armies were fighting in these regions. In addition to the important cupola composition, the main two-sided altar, serving both the Soldiers'

Figure 78. Jules Hardouin-Mansart, Dôme of the Invalides, Paris, 1677–1706.   Exterior.   (Photo: Author.)

Figure 79. Jules Hardouin-Mansart, Dôme of the Invalides, Paris, 1677–1706. Interior. (Photo: Archives Photographiques, Paris/S.P.A.D.E.M.)

Church and the Dôme, was at first projected as an open columnar structure, its upper part decorated with palm branches topped by a royal crown, the former a symbol of both Christian victory over death and military triumph, the latter a reminder of the royal nature of the building. The exterior dome (Fig. 78) was decorated (1691–2) with gilded military trophies, announcing the martial theme from afar. We know that the model of the church with La Fosse's painting was shown to the King and the Court in February 1677.

Hardouin-Mansart was able to quickly produce the basic design for the Dôme in the spring of 1676 by utilizing his great-uncle's unrealized drawings of ca. 1662–4 for a royal Bourbon mausoleum to be appended to the venerable burial church of French kings, the basilica of Saint-Denis. (Hardouin-Mansart had access to these drawings, kept under lock and key in the Mansart family, by a special legal agreement drawn up in 1666 after the death of François.) One of these sheets (Fig. 81) shows a central plan building with a large domed circular area in the center surrounded by chapels on the cross axes, with crossing piers cut through by passages leading to corner chapels. Hardouin-Mansart suppressed the protruding chapels and inscribed the whole within a square, with only slight projections on the flanks of the cubic body of the building; the corner chapels were regularized with circular plans (cf. Fig. 75). For the interior elevation of the Dôme of the Invalides, the younger Mansart followed his great-uncle's sketches on the same sheet even more faithfully: a comparison of sectional views of the Dôme (Figs. 82 and 83) and the executed crossing (Fig. 79) with François Mansart's section at the left reveals the same very vertical proportions; the main story with its tall order, full entablature, and pierced crossing piers with columns framing false-perspective arches (note Mansart's separate sketch of this detail above the left-hand section); the next level with its broad-footed pendentives and semicircular arches opening into the barrel-vaulted arms; and, finally, the great crossing with its windowed drum supporting a cupola with a very wide oculus that permits a view of a higher cupola, all contained within the exterior shell with its pointed profile, supported by a secondary drum with volute buttresses, this in turn resting on the main drum with columns and entablature.

At the end of the 1680s, as the body of the great building was nearing completion, Hardouin-Mansart revised the dome by piercing the upper, secondary drum with a ring of large windows (cf. Figs. 82 and 83), a feature faintly suggested by the elder Mansart (Fig. 81, section at right). These windows provide light for the painted decoration of the upper cupola (Fig. 80), the light falling upon it by means of openings in that cupola that cannot be seen by the spectator standing below on the floor of the church. (It was upon this upper cupola that La Fosse intended to paint the composition discussed earlier.) This lighting system – proposed before in 1683/4 by

Mansart for an unrealized central-plan chapel for the Château of Versailles (Fig. 110) – is a monumental example of hidden illumination, a feature of Baroque art pioneered earlier in the century in the chapels and churches of Bernini.

This Baroque dome was eventually capped by an open lantern and spire (Fig. 78), the former derived from a design (ca. 1645–6) for the Parisian church of the Val-de-Grâce by François Mansart. However, the interior of the Dôme of the Invalides – with its magnificent Corinthian order of fluted columns and pilasters and complex, broken entablature with curved segments set against the crossing piers (Fig. 79) – seems like the realization of an ideal central-plan (Greek cross) church of the Italian High Renaissance. From a central point beneath the cupola, the viewer could enjoy views in all directions, the pierced crossing piers allowing for deep, diagonal vistas into the corner chapels, and this visibility is enhanced by views from one peripheral space to another. The monumental two-story entrance façade (Fig. 78), with its Roman Doric order surmounted by a Corinthian order above, jogs forward from its planar edges through framed, windowed bays and then to columns in two planes culminating in a pedimented temple-front motif. Not indicated by the elder Mansart, this façade is an original contribution of his great-nephew.

The Dôme of the Invalides, begun in 1677, took many years to complete and was not finally consecrated until 1706 (work continued into 1709). During this long construction period, progressive changes were made in its decorative program. As the fortune of French arms decreased during Louis XIV's later wars, the emphasis changed from a temple of martial glory to a religious shrine that stressed the sainted Louis IX, the French king with whom Louis XIV was increasingly associated in the later years of his reign. A statue of the saint appears in the left-hand niche of the main façade, along with Charlemagne's in the right-hand one (Fig. 78; cf. also Fig. 3, where the two earlier kings appear). Within, the painting of the upper cupola, again entrusted to La Fosse, was changed to a scene of the reception of Saint Louis into Heaven (Fig. 80), with the saint presenting his sword to Christ. The lower, cutoff dome, earlier projected with medallions of French rulers and then with angels, was finally painted with the twelve apostles between coffered ribs (by Jean Jouvenet) (Fig. 80). Smaller sculpted medallions of the French kings (including Louis XIV) now appear at the base of the drum (Figs. 79 and 80), and bas-reliefs with scenes from the life of Saint Louis appear at strategic locations in the interior. The high altar – a baldachin of six spiral columns recalling both Bernini's famous canopy in St. Peter's and the one in the Val-de-Grâce by French designers (1664) – was in the end dedicated to Saint Louis, and by 1686 (according to the *Mercure galant*), the arch behind it had been so built that the altar could be fully viewed

Figure 80. Jules Hardouin-Mansart, Dôme of the Invalides, Paris, 1677–1706. View of Cupola. (Photo: Caisse Nationale des Monuments Historiques et des Sites, Paris/ S.P.A.D.E.M.)

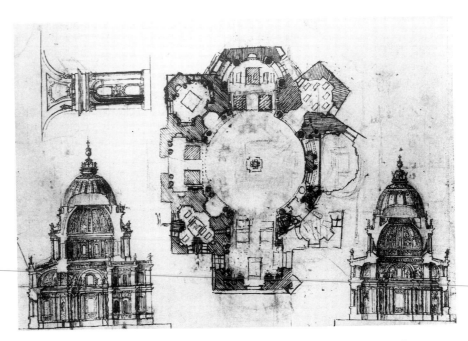

Figure 81. François Mansart, Design for the Bourbon Chapel, Saint-Denis. Drawing, ca. 1662–4. Bibliothèque Nationale, Paris, Cabinet des Estampes. (Photo: from A. Braham and P. Smith, *François Mansart,* II, London, 1973.)

Figure 82. Office of Jules Hardouin-Mansart, Dôme of the Invalides, Paris, 1677–1706. Section. Drawing, Bibliothèque Nationale, Paris, Cabinet des Estampes. (Photo: Bibliothèque Nationale, Paris.)

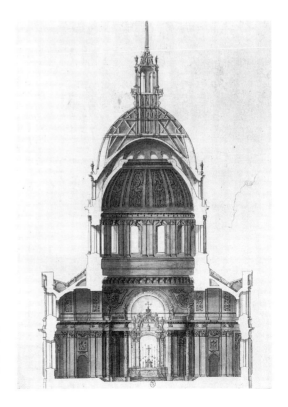

Figure 83. Office of Jules Hardouin-Mansart, Dôme of the Invalides, Paris, 1677–1706. Section. Drawing, Bibliothèque Nationale, Paris, Cabinet des Estampes. (Photo: Bibliothèque Nationale, Paris.)

Figure 84. Gobelins Tapestry after Pierre Dulin, *Louis XIV and Louvois Establishing the Invalides*, woven after 1710. Mobilier National, Paris. (Photo: Mobilier National.)

from the Soldiers' Church. (The present baldachin is a nineteenth-century replacement, and the interior space has been irrevocably marred by the cutting of a huge hole in the center of the floor [Fig. 79] to allow viewing of Napoleon's tomb in a crypt below [1843–61].)

When Mansart first presented his scheme for the Dôme of the Invalides in 1676, he envisaged an oval public square before the building, but it was not further articulated on paper until ca. 1698–1702. Mansart was obviously thinking of Bernini's Piazza of St. Peter's in the Vatican, but with emphatic domed end pavilions framing curved arcaded segments. The project was never executed, probably for financial reasons.

The decision of 1676 to create a double church, with one serving as a retrochoir for the soldiers, the other as a huge temple for the public, celebrating the military glory of France, must have been formulated at first in the highest royal and official levels. It is doubtful that Hardouin-Mansart spontaneously proposed the idea. There must have been preliminary discussions between the King, Louvois, perhaps Colbert, court intellectuals, and the Petite Académie in working out the basic program of the Invalides complex; unfortunately, no trace of these deliberations has survived. A Gobelins tapestry (Fig. 84) (based on Pierre Dulin's late painting of 1710), although containing allegorical figures, shows the Marquis de Louvois explaining the plan of the Invalides to the King; it is a reminder of conferences that surely took place (and which of course included Mansart), and also of the constant interest of the Sun King in this vast, functional, but also powerfully symbolic project.

The Dôme of the Invalides was not consecrated until August 1706, twenty-nine years after it was begun (see Chap. 16). The long-awaited event was duly reported at length in the September issue of the *Mercure galant*, which went on to make some interesting comments about the artistic significance of the church, comments that related directly to the Quarrel of the Ancients and Moderns that raged throughout most of the Ludovican period (Chap. 1):

Whatever may be said by all those who praise antiquity, it is impossible that it ever attained the perfection that is found today in all the works where the arts have some share; since most of the arts that serve to perfect everything we see today of the greatest beauty had not then been invented, and those that have been [invented] since those times have scarcely attained complete perfection. The wonders of the world that have been praised in all centuries have been [praised] less for the delicacy and beauty of their workmanship than for the immensity of their scale, in which their rarest qualities are found. It is necessary that today's works of art be composed of a great number of different parts, which, in their kind, are as many different masterpieces; it is this that makes one admire the church of the Invalides, which the architect has fashioned to receive all the ornaments that the fine arts can lend to this great edifice.

The anonymous writer's use of the word "délicatesse" has a special Gallic resonance that recalls a recurrent French aesthetic preference through the ages. To be sure, the Dôme is a building that in no way resembles the architecture of ancient Greece or Rome, and the *Mercure* states that it, like other contemporary buildings, is more complex, made up of parts adorned by painting, sculpture, and gilding: "so many beauties [put] together must produce a marvellous sight, capable of enchanting all viewers."

Late in the Sun King's reign, then, his largest and most costly Parisian church was taken as offering proof of the victory of the Moderns over the Ancients. The same triumph is implied by a contemporary phenomenon in interior decoration – the development of the Rococo around the year 1700 (Chap. 10), a style that owes nothing to the classical tradition. The Moderns of the age of Louis XIV triumphed not by outrivaling antiquity at its own game, but by producing a new, original architecture. Although French architects much earlier in the reign had invented a palace façade – the Louvre Colonnade (Fig. 23; Chap. 4) – that perhaps resembles ancient classical architecture more closely than anything ever erected since the fall of the Roman empire, the building was stoutly defended by Claude Perrault, at least, as a triumph of the Moderns because the coupled columns produced a new type of intercolumniation unknown to the Ancients. Perrault's opponent in the debate was Blondel of the Royal Academy of Architecture, who sharply criticized the paired columns, the overall proportions ("dwarfish and crushed"), and the use of iron (proof of flawed masonry construction), judging the Colonnade a failure that only vindicated the eternal supremacy of Greece and Rome. But this façade, although judged a masterpiece by most contemporaries, exerted very little influence. Rather, it was the adjoining south front of the Louvre (Fig. 27), derived from the Italian Renaissance and not at all antique, that was frequently used as a model. The age of Neoclassicism had not yet arrived. Molière had caught the real temper of the times in his lines from *The Imaginary Invalid* (see Chap. 1).

VERSAILLES – II (1678–1715)

A new phase of activity at Versailles began in 1678 with the ascendancy there of Hardouin-Mansart, who replaced d'Orbay as chief architect of the château. Still in the midst of ongoing work at Clagny and the Invalides (Chaps. 8 and 9), Mansart organized a team of assistants (including d'Orbay on occasion) who aided him in designing an enormous body of work for a Versailles that was soon to be proclaimed (1682) the new royal capital. In 1681, Mansart was appointed first architect of the King, filling a post that had been vacant since the death of Louis Le Vau in 1670.

In preparation for its new role, Versailles, beginning in 1678, was transformed by Mansart into a gigantic, unified creation, unprecedented in scale, a new architectural archetype for the age of absolutism (Fig. 85). The château sprouted enormous wings to house the expanded population of the court, with the Envelope elevation repeated on the garden side, a sober brick-and-stone design facing the town (south wing, 1678–82, Fig. 88; north wing, 1684/5–9). The wings accentuated the north–south garden axis that passed in front of the western façade of the Envelope, and this axis was prolonged to the north by the Neptune Basin (1679–85) and, especially, to the south by a gigantic man-made lake, the Pièce d'Eau des Suisses (the Water Basin of the Swiss, referring to the mercenary soldiers who dug it). From 1681 to 1685, Mansart rebuilt Le Vau's brick-and-stone orangery entirely in stone and doubled its size, with the central *allée* of its garden now aligned on the north–south axis (Fig. 88). When seen from the south, especially from the end of the Pièce d'Eau des Suisses, the Orangerie with its gigantic flanking Cent Marches (Hundred Steps) appears as a pedestal for the palace – a truly grand view (Fig. 90). Mansart's Orangerie was extravagantly praised as one of the architectural marvels not simply of Versailles, but of the world. Contemporaries admired both its huge size and, surprisingly, its austerity, inside and out, which permits the patterns and volumes

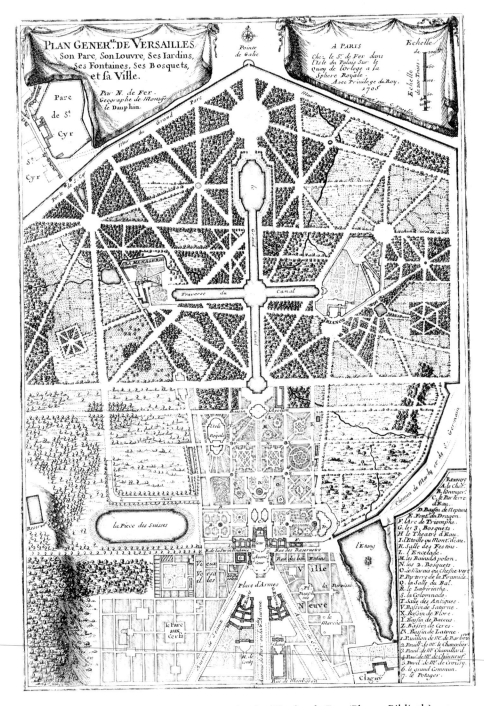

Figure 85. Plan of Versailles, 1705. Engraving by Nicolas de Fer. (Photo: Bibliothèque Nationale, Paris.)

Figure 86. Pierre-Denis Martin, *Entrance View of Versailles,* 1722. Musée National du Château de Versailles. (Photo: Réunion des Musées Nationaux.)

Figure 87. Jean-Baptiste Martin, *View of the Courtyard and Stables of Versailles,* ca. 1690. Musée National du Château de Versailles. (Photo: Réunion des Musées Nationaux.)

Figure 88. Jules Hardouin-Mansart, Orangerie (1681–5) and South Wing of the Château (1678–82), Versailles. (Photo: Réunion des Musées Nationaux.)

of the stonework (stereotomy) to be clearly studied. On the exterior (Fig. 88), the height between horizontal grooves equals one module, or one-half the diameter of a column (connoisseurs of the period were sensitive to these measurements, derived from antique architectural practice); inside (Fig. 89), barrel-vaulted galleries, entirely undecorated, remind one of Perrault's aesthetic in the Observatoire (Figs. 35, 36). The *Mercure galant* in 1686 specifically praised the interior of the Orangerie for its decorum (see Chap. 1), stating that "The interior is not adorned with any sculpture or architecture [i.e., architectural decoration], as this type of building requires, and the contrivance of the vaults creates the greatest beauty."

Mansart's growing power in the artistic hierarchy began to encroach upon Le Nôtre's domain during the 1680s. A Parterre d'Eau (water parterre) of complex plan, set before the western façade of the palace, was entirely refashioned beginning in 1683/4 to Mansart's simplified design, with two serene oblong basins flanking the east–west garden axis, their long axes stressing that axis (Fig. 91). The rims of the basins were adorned with the extant reclining bronze statues of river gods, representing the main rivers of France (castings finished in 1690). Additional *bosquets* were built in the Petit Parc, including the Colonnade (1684–8/9; Fig. 92), a design that reveals Mansart's tendency to insert architectural forms within the garden itself, a procedure that angered Le Nôtre and provoked him to comment sarcastically to the King in the presence of courtiers. The Colonnade was

Figure 89. Jules Hardouin-Mansart, Orangerie, Versailles, 1681–5. Interior. (Photo: from C. Mauricheau-Beaupré, *Versailles*, Monaco, 1949.)

Figure 90. Pièce d'Eau des Suisses, Versailles, begun 1679. (Photo: Author.)

Figure 91. Jules Hardouin-Mansart, Parterre d'Eau, Versailles, begun 1683/4. (Photo: Author.)

Figure 92. Jules Hardouin-Mansart, Colonnade, Versailles, 1684–8/9. (Photo: Réunion des Musées Nationaux.)

intended to glorify Louis: the marble bas-reliefs of children at play in its spandrels refer to the peace that he had brought to France after the Dutch War of the 1670s, and the marble group of *The Fame of Louis XIV* by the Italian sculptor Domenico Guidi was later intended to stand at its center (never placed). In the airy lightness of its forms, the Colonnade prefigured the coming Rococo style.

Hardouin-Mansart's assumption of architectural power at Versailles beginning in 1678 was surely due to the King's confidence in him gained at Clagny and the Invalides. At those projects, Mansart was dealing with Louis XIV via Madame de Montespan and Louvois; Colbert, for once, was on the sidelines. There seems to have been a personal chemistry between Louis and Mansart, reminiscent of the King and Bernini. An apocryphal anecdote about how Louis "discovered" the architect, then a mere mason, stresses how the Monarch recognized Mansart's political tact in erasing an architectural drawing because it might have aroused the envy of his colleagues and master. As a compliment to the young man, the King is said to have traced the same design with his cane in the sand. The story seems to allude to Mansart's unquestionable later abilities as a courtier, which the King must have deeply appreciated.

A visit to Versailles demanded a tour of the gardens, and between 1689 and 1705 Louis XIV himself drew up several brief itineraries, which he called the *Manière de montrer les jardins de Versailles* (Manner of showing the gardens of Versailles). One of the versions survives in the King's handwriting, and another, in the hand of a secretary, bears corrections by Louis in the margins. The itineraries were meant for officials in charge of conducting visitors of distinction through the gardens; exceptionally, this might be done by the King himself. The style of the *Manière* is dry and laconic; consider the beginning of the 1694 redaction:

1. Upon leaving the château by the vestibule of the Marble Court, one will proceed to the terrace; one must halt at the top of the steps to view the arrangement of the water *parterres* [Fig. 91] and the fountains of the cabinets [of the animals].
2. One must then proceed straight to the height overlooking Latona and pause to view Latona, the Lizards, the ramps, the statues, the royal *allée*, Apollo, the canal [Figs. 42 and 43], and then turn around to see the [water] *parterres* and the château [Fig. 52].

The promenade, then, followed a prescribed route, with pauses at determined viewing points. Occasionally, the King specified what the visitor should especially notice, as in the instructions of 1694 for visiting the Colonnade (Fig. 92), where "one shall proceed to the center, where one shall make a tour to view the columns, the arches, the bas-reliefs, and the basins. Upon leaving, one shall halt to view the group by Guidi . . ." [*The Fame of Louis XIV*, then standing at the entrance to the *bosquet*].

Figure 93. Aqueduct, Maintenon, 1685–8. (Photo: Author.)

In order to furnish his garden with more water (an endemic problem), Louis XIV had built, from 1681–4, the so-called Machine de Marly, which brought up water from the Seine for the two royal châteaux (for Marly, see Chap. 11). To supplement the Machine, the King in 1684 ordered his fortifications engineer, the Marquis de Vauban (Chap. 13), to design an aqueduct to bring the waters of the Eure River to Versailles. Vauban wanted to construct an inclined open trench, but the King and Louvois insisted on a monumental three-tiered arcuated construction, perhaps consciously thought of as a rival to the Pont du Gard, which had impressed Louis in his youth. In the event, the work, started in 1685 on the grounds of Madame de Maintenon's estate, not far from Chartres, by a work force of tens of thousands, was interrupted in 1688 by the outbreak of war and never resumed (Fig. 93). Versailles remained with an insufficient water supply.

On the town side before the château (Fig. 86), Mansart, in a brilliant stroke, filled in the wedge-shaped spaces between the converging avenues with the royal stables (Grande and Petite Écuries, 1679–82; Fig. 87), shaped in plan like horseshoes or magnets with converging sides that point toward the château. The stables, the wings, the new water basins, and the Orangerie all serve to accentuate major axial and directional relationships in the total plan of Versailles – testimony to Mansart's large-scale thinking.

From the period 1678–1715, three great enterprises, all linked to Mansart, call for detailed discussion: the Galerie des Glaces, the Grand or Marble Trianon, and the chapel. These projects, like everything else at Versailles, were of the highest interest and importance to Louis XIV, and he participated in their realization on a daily basis.

GALERIE DES GLACES

By 1678, on the eve of the expansion of Versailles under Mansart, Louis XIV must have realized that the château lacked an appropriate long gallery, unlike the situation at the Louvre where the Galerie d'Apollon proclaimed the King's power, wealth, and artistic taste (Fig. 15). The Petit Château lacked a long gallery, and Le Vau's Envelope only contained a low and narrow one on the ground floor (the Galerie Basse). What was needed was a long gallery on the first floor, where the Monarch lived and ceremonial life took place. Early in 1678, the decision was made to destroy Le Vau's western terrace and adjoining rooms (Figs. 49 and 51) and create an enclosed gallery in their place, flanked by the corner rooms of the Envelope. Work began later that year, and by 1681, the gallery was ready to be painted. It is possible that Louis was impelled in this enterprise by the example of his brother's château at Saint-Cloud, which contained a monumental long gallery, painted by Pierre Mignard in 1677–8.

The creation of the Galerie des Glaces (Hall of Mirrors) at Versailles resulted in a straight garden façade with a new central *avant-corps* with six free-standing columns (Figs. 52 and 94). Mansart designed the gallery to be covered with a barrel vault of wood, supported from above by a truss. This construction can be seen in Figure 95, a sectional view of 1678. The drawing clearly shows that the top-floor windows of Mansart's revised Envelope are sham openings. The light tunnels proposed were never built because it was soon decided to sheath the entire long inner wall of the gallery with mirrors, the motif that gives the room its name (*glace* = plate glass) (Fig. 96). It was probably during 1678–9 that Le Brun prepared drawings for an Apollo cycle for the room, and it is possible that the mirrors were thought of as a means of increased luminosity, appropriate for the painted theme. They were retained, however, even after the Apollo cycle was rejected in favor of new ideas. Additional light was brought into the gallery and all the outer rooms of the Envelope by changing Le Vau's straight-headed windows into semicircular-arched ones.

In working out the architectural decoration of the gallery, Mansart

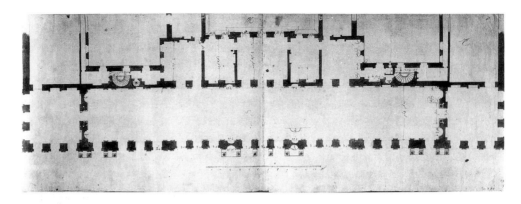

Figure 94. Office of Jules Hardouin-Mansart, Galerie des Glaces, Versailles, Plan. Drawing, 1678. Louvre, Paris, Cabinet des Dessins. (Photo: Réunion des Musées Nationaux.)

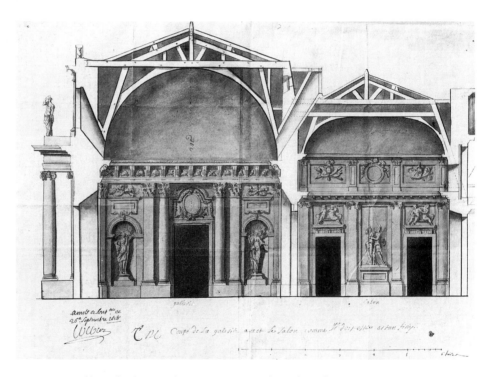

Figure 95. Office of Jules Hardouin-Mansart, Galerie des Glaces, Section. Drawing, 1678. Louvre, Paris, Cabinet des Dessins. (Photo: Réunion des Musées Nationaux.)

worked hand in glove with Le Brun, the first painter. Le Brun's "French" order, a variation on the Corinthian, articulates the long and end walls, and proclaims French national pride, as does the domestically made (non-Venetian) glass and native French purplish marble, which forms a rich contrast with the lavishly gilded moldings. Niches on the long wall held

Figure 96. Jules Hardouin-Mansart, Galerie des Glaces, Versailles, 1678–84. (Photo: Alinari-Giraudon/Art Resource, New York.)

Figure 97. Antoine Coypel, *Reception of the Persian Ambassadors (1715).* Musée National du Château de Versailles. (Photo: Réunion des Musées Nationaux.)

choice antique statues from the royal collection, thus continuing one of the traditional uses of the long gallery. The ceiling paintings by Le Brun and his studio that fill the vault are the result of several changes of program. The original Apollo cycle project was superseded by one dedicated to Hercules (Louis XIV's other *persona*), in turn rejected in favor of the executed decorations (1681–4), mainly depicting events from the just-concluded Dutch War, with contemporary personages accompanied by classical deities and personifications. As in the Galerie d'Apollon at the Louvre (Fig. 15), the vault was divided into a number of compartments, with the Dutch War scenes occupying the larger ones. The tone of the imagery is aggressive both visually and thematically, with numerous figures in complex actions portraying the defeat of France's enemies by the Sun King, aided by divine powers. The gallery is preceded at each end by the Salon de la Guerre and Salon de la Paix (Salon of War and Salon of Peace, painted 1684–7), occupying the former Salons of Jupiter (King's and Queen's side) at the corners of the Envelope. These rooms also display the mirror motif of the gallery along with vaults painted by Le Brun and his assistants.

The Galerie des Glaces was, of course, intended to astonish visitors and intimidate foreign ambassadors (Fig. 97), and this it accomplished merely because it was the largest long gallery yet built (73 meters long, 40 meters wide, 13 meters to the top of the vault). Its triumphant ceiling paintings recount French military power, and two guidebooks (1684, 1687), which explain these paintings in great detail, are said to have been expressly ordered by the King himself. But the uniqueness of the room also derived from the use of glass on an unprecedented scale, and this may have been a gesture meant to surpass a famous reception hall of the Spanish enemy, the Salon de los Espejos (Salon of Mirrors) in the old Alcázar of Madrid, a room that featured pairs of large mirrors on its shorter walls facing each other (a decoration of the 1640s). In the seventeenth century, political rivalries were not confined to battlefields, but could find architectural expression as well.

GRAND TRIANON (TRIANON DE MARBRE)

We recall that Le Vau's Trianon de Porcelaine (see Chap. 6; Fig. 56) – the first "Chinese" building in Western architecture – had a roof decorated with ceramic ornaments. These had proven vulnerable to the weather, and, probably for this reason, the structure was dismantled in 1687. It was swiftly replaced by the extant Grand or Marble Trianon, another creation of the new first architect, Hardouin-Mansart (Figs. 102–5). It is invariably assumed that in building this new Trianon (finished by the end of 1687), all Chinese associations were abandoned. But this may not have been the case. What is immediately striking about the new structure is its very low, essentially one-story character. Its predecessor was also of one floor, but the Grand Trianon celebrates, as it were, this quality by its sprawling plan and lack of visible roofs. It is interesting to note that seventeenth-century descriptions of Chinese architecture made a point of the lack of higher stories. The Jesuit Athanasius Kircher, whose *China monumentis* of 1667 appeared in a French translation in 1670, wrote

Concerning the architecture of houses, I will tell you that they do not build them so much for magnificence and glory as for the convenience [*la commodité*] of the inhabitants. They almost all have only one story; because the *Chinese* never want to mount or descend stairs. That is why they make the length of their houses substitute for the height of our edifices.

The Grand Trianon lacked the pseudo-orientalizing motifs present in its predecessor, both within and without, but an exotic allusion may have been subtly preserved through its overall design.

Like the Trianon de Porcelaine, the Marble Trianon was intended for the King's relaxation. It was provided with separate apartments for His Majesty and his morganatic wife, Madame de Maintenon, and her court ladies, but these rooms were more for display (*appartements d'apparat*) than for sleeping. Extensive kitchens were installed around a service court behind the left wing, and after 1692 a small theater was created within the right one (Fig. 100), thus indicating some of the principal pleasures that Trianon afforded.

Several features of the Grand Trianon embody some very specific wishes of the King, and demonstrate his very active role in the genesis of the building; they will be discussed in Chapter 14. Here we should note the boldly asymmetrical plan, formed by a long gallery (Fig. 100) that links the main body of the building with a separate wing called "Trianon-sous-Bois" (Trianon-under-the-Trees), which, in its original form (Fig. 101), extended the one-story theme (it was remodeled into the present two-story appendage by Mansart in 1705–6; Fig. 109). Here were provided apartments (which could be lived in for brief periods) for the King's brother, his wife, and family.

The flower garden of the Porcelain Trianon was preserved, and the new building was designed to effect a union between architecture and surrounding nature in a manner not attempted in the preceding structure. Thus, the central open portico, or peristyle (Fig. 105), linking the two L-shaped *corps-de-logis*, allows the visitor entering the central courtyard to glimpse the garden behind the building (Fig. 102). This was noted in a text of 1689, written immediately after the building was completed:

The glitter of the marbles and the beauties of the architecture at first fix the view on that great façade called the peristyle; and the pleasure redoubles when, by the

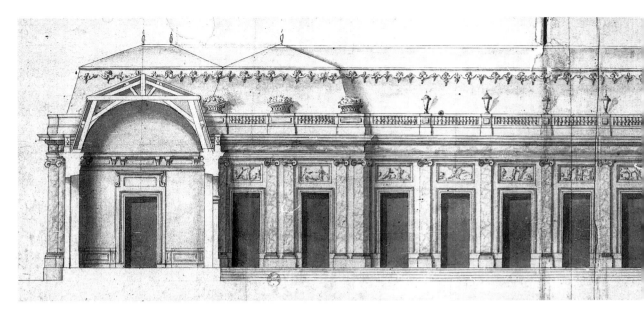

Figure 98. Office of Jules Hardouin-Mansart, Initial Design for the Grand Trianon, Versailles, Section and Elevation. Drawing, 1687. Bibliothèque Nationale, Paris, Cabinet des Estampes. (Photo: Bibliothèque Nationale, Paris.)

Figure 99. Office of Jules Hardouin-Mansart, Initial Design for the Grand Trianon, Versailles, Plan. Drawing, 1687. Bibliothèque Nationale, Paris, Cabinet des Estampes. (Photo: from A. Marie and J. Marie, *Versailles au temps de Louis XIV,* Paris, 1976.)

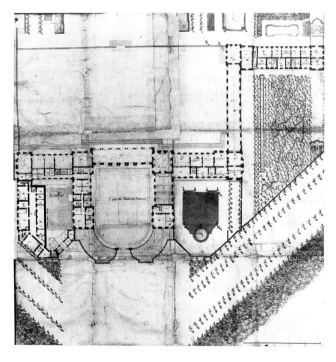

Figure 100. Office of Jules Hardouin-Mansart, Grand Trianon, Versailles, Final Plan. Drawing, 1687. Bibliothèque Nationale, Paris, Cabinet des Estampes. (Photo: Bibliothèque Nationale, Paris.)

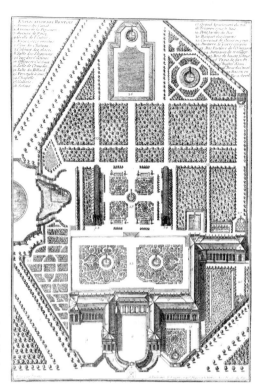

Figure 101. Jules Hardouin-Mansart, Grand Trianon, Versailles, 1687. Bird's-Eye View. Engraving by Nicolas Langlois after Perelle. (Photo: Bibliothèque Nationale, Paris.)

Figure 102. Jules Hardouin-Mansart, Grand Trianon, Versailles, 1687. Entrance Façade. (Photo: J. Feuillie/Caisse Nationale des Monuments Historiques et des Sites, Paris/S.P.A.D.E.M.)

Figure 103. Jules Hardouin-Mansart, Grand Trianon, Versailles, 1687. Garden Façade. (Photo: Author.)

Figure 104. Jules Hardouin-Mansart, Grand Trianon, Versailles, 1687. Garden Façade. (Photo: Author.)

Figure 105. Jules Hardouin-Mansart, Grand Trianon, Versailles, 1687. Peristyle. (Photo: Giraudon/Art Resource.)

openings of its arcades, between several ranges of rich columns, one glimpses those fountains, those gardens, and those *parterres* always filled with all sorts of flowers.

The themes of Flora, spring, and the Loves of the Gods (traditionally associated with flowers and springtime) appeared in various guises in almost 160 mythological, topographical, and still-life paintings for the interiors, commissioned beginning in 1688. In one of these pictures, by Jean Cotelle the Younger (Fig. 106), the Grand Trianon is seen from the garden, with a view of the flowered *parterres,* central water basin, and the diaphanous portico, through which are glimpsed the trees of the park of Versailles. The goddess Flora sleeps in the foreground, attended by her nymphs while Zephyr hovers amorously overhead, forming an allegory of eternal spring, which was the season that contemporaries felt themselves to be in whenever they were at Trianon.

A conscious attempt to link indoors and outdoors in a new, more intimate manner is clearly revealed in a document of 1694 by Le Nôtre, written one year after his official retirement. The royal gardener explained that certain fountains had been sited to be seen from particular rooms. Thus, the Salon des Jardins, located at the far end of the long gallery adjacent to Trianon-sous-Bois (Figs. 100 and 101), looked out on a large rectangular water basin with jet. The long rectangular basin near it with several jets in a row was meant to be seen from Trianon-sous-Bois. At the near end of the long gallery, from the Salon des Sources, a shell fountain at the end of a walk came into view. All of these garden features had been designed by Le Nôtre, working in close harmony with Hardouin-Mansart (despite their strained professional relationship). For the Salon des Sources (Salon of the Springs), the painter René-Antoine Houasse created three mythological canvases depicting water themes: *Narcissus Looking at his Reflexion, The Nymph Cyanee Changed into a Fountain,* and *Alpheus and Arethusa;* thus, the interior decoration complemented the view of the fountain. The inhabitants of the Grand Trianon appreciated this newly accentuated closeness to nature; Philippe's second wife, Élisabeth-Charlotte von der Pfalz, wrote in 1705 from her room in Trianon-sous-Bois that "the trees almost enter my windows."

Trianon was thus a laboratory for experiments in the relationship of architecture to its surroundings and in garden design itself. In the space formed by the angle of the long gallery with Trianon-sous-Bois, Le Nôtre created a miniature protoromantic garden, Les Sources (The Springs) (1687) (Fig. 107). It consisted of irregularly planted trees and a network of twisting, meandering rivulets. In his *mémoire* of 1694, Le Nôtre wrote that Les Sources was

filled with a full-grown wood whose trees are separated one from another, which has allowed for the creation of small canals that go serpenting without order and turn in empty spaces around the trees with irregularly-placed water jets. . . .

I cannot write you enough about the beauty of this place: it has a coolness where the ladies go to work, play, take a light meal, and [enjoy] the beauty of the site; you enter it directly from [Trianon-sous-Bois]; thus from that apartment you go under shade through all the various beauties. . . . I can say that it is the only garden, along with the Tuileries, that I know to be easy to walk in and the most beautiful. I leave the others in their beauty and grandeur, but [it is] the most comfortable.

We should note Le Nôtre's mention of nonclassical features like serpentine form and irregularity. Les Sources, alas, was destroyed at the beginning of the nineteenth century, and only old plans hint at its appearance. It existed throughout the eighteenth century, an available stimulus for English visitors seeking a new garden aesthetic. (For more on the Grand Trianon, see Chapter 14.)

Figure 106. Jean Cotelle the Younger, *View of Grand Trianon, Versailles (Zephyr and Flora),* ca. 1690. Grand Trianon, Versailles. (Photo: Réunion des Musées Nationaux.)

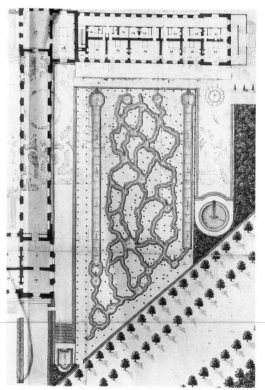

Figure 107. André Le Nôtre, Garden of Les Sources, Grand Trianon, Versailles, 1687. Plan (detail). Drawing, Bibliothèque Nationale, Paris, Cabinet des Estampes. (Photo: Bibliothèque Nationale, Paris.)

Figure 108. Jules Hardouin-Mansart, Grand Trianon, Versailles, 1687. Gallery. (Photo: J. Feuillie/Caisse Nationale des Monuments Historiques et des Sites, Paris/ S.P.A.D.E.M.)

Figure 109. Jules Hardouin-Mansart, Trianon-sous-Bois, Grand Trianon, Versailles, 1705–6. (Photo: Author.)

THE CHAPEL

The history of the Château of Versailles reveals that six successive chapels were arranged or expressly built for it, two within the Petit Château, two within the south range of the Envelope, the fifth adjacent to it to the north. It is the sixth chapel, by far the largest and most elaborate, that survives today (Figs. 113–15). Generally regarded as a great and unique masterpiece, the building is the result of a particularly interesting design chronicle.

From the early 1680s on, Louis XIV became more outwardly religious, due at least in part to the influence of a new and pious mistress, Madame de Maintenon, whom he secretly wed in a morganatic marriage in 1684, the year following the death of Queen Marie-Thérèse. The King's new religiosity coincided with fresh persecutions (*dragonnades*) of Protestants and, in 1685, with the Revocation of the Edict of Nantes, which withdrew the toleration of the Huguenots that had existed from the time of Henry IV.

In the midst of this atmosphere, in 1683/4, Hardouin-Mansart and Charles Le Brun (who occasionally practiced architecture) were asked for designs for a new Versailles chapel. Mansart's proposal was favored and designs from his office (one is shown in Fig. 110) were published in 1684 as a series of engravings. These showed a domed church of Greek-cross plan with corner chapels, located in the center of a new north wing, the latter begun in December of that year. Mansart's design was closely based upon his Dôme of the Invalides, designed in 1676 and then rising (Chap. 9). The tall drum and dome of his project for Versailles would have appeared above the rooflines of the north wing, an unavoidable object when viewed either from the town or the gardens. This conspicuousness would have marked the domed church off from all previous chapels at Versailles.

No action was taken on Mansart's proposal, however. Several years passed that saw continued construction of the north wing. Then, in late 1688 or very early in 1689, the first architect submitted a new chapel design of radically different form (Fig. 111). Not located like its predecessor in the center of the new wing, but rather closer to the château itself (and hence nearer to the King's living quarters), the new design featured a rectangular plan with a vaulted nave flanked by aisles, a semicircular apse and ambulatory, and a tripartite interior elevation of semicircular arches on stout piers (ground floor), a somewhat higher tribune story above (for the King) with Corinthian pilasters (schematically rendered in Fig. 111) decorating thinner piers with arches, and a clerestory. An exterior elevation shows two lower stories meant to harmonize with the north wing elevation in floor heights and articulation, and a distinct clerestory level with a low pitched roof.

This exterior with, be it noted, flying buttresses at clerestory level (indicated at the left edge of Fig. 111) surprisingly recalls the royal French palace chapels in Gothic style of Saint-Germain-en-Laye (1230–8), the Sainte-Chapelle in Paris (1243–6; Fig. 117), and the chapel at Vincennes (1379–mid-sixteenth century). Clearly, a high-level decision had been made to reject the Italianate domed project and to substitute a design that, while almost entirely classical in its detailing, could take its place in a native royal French Gothic tradition. Mansart's solution may have been intended as an architectural statement of Gallicanism (the policy of according the French king and clergy certain powers not subject to papal control), but it may also reflect the stimulus of a very recent book (1687) by Jean-François Félibien (the son of André, the historiographer of the royal buildings), which included a pioneering attempt to write a history of medieval architecture and which bestowed praise upon the three royal chapels cited before. The new Versailles chapel was to be dedicated to Saint Louis IX, who in fact was the builder of both the chapel at Saint-Germain and the Sainte-Chapelle. (On Louis XIV's association with Saint Louis, see Chapter 9.) In January 1689, Mansart showed his design to the Royal Academy of Architecture, which approved the unclassical, Gothic proportions of the nave, the height of which exceeded twice its width.

Work on the foundations and ground-floor arches was begun in 1689 but then halted that year because of funding problems caused by the War of the League of Augsburg (1688–97). After the return of peace, the King ordered a resumption of the chapel in December 1698. Another drawing from Mansart's office (Fig. 112), probably dating from that month, reveals significant changes. The polychrome marble revetment of the earlier project is retained, but the royal tribune level is now appreciably higher than the arcaded ground floor and – most important – slender free-standing Corinthian columns carrying a straight entablature have replaced pilasters set against piers supporting arches. The interior space of the nave is even more verticalized, and on the exterior, the sloped roof is much higher and steeper. The interior elevation with arcades surmounted by a royal tribune level distinguished by columns probably was meant to recall another medieval building, Charlemagne's Palatine Chapel at Aix-la-Chapelle (now Aachen, Germany) (Fig. 118), which was also part of a royal palace complex. Thus, the Versailles chapel linked Louis XIV to the two sainted French kings, Charlemagne and Louis IX, whose statues, we recall, decorate the façade of the Dôme of the Invalides (Fig. 78). (Charlemagne was canonized in 1165 by the antipope Pascal III, but his sainthood was never recognized subsequently by the Holy See; his public cult, however, was tolerated in France and Germany.) In January 1699, the idea of a polychrome marble interior was discarded in favor of white stone (Fig. 114). Health reasons were cited for this, but it is also true that marble polychromy was out of fashion by 1699 and was more expensive than stone.

Figure 110. Office of Jules Hardouin-Mansart, Central-Plan Design for Versailles Chapel, Section. Drawing, 1683/4. National-museum, Stockholm. (Photo: Statens Konstmuseer.)

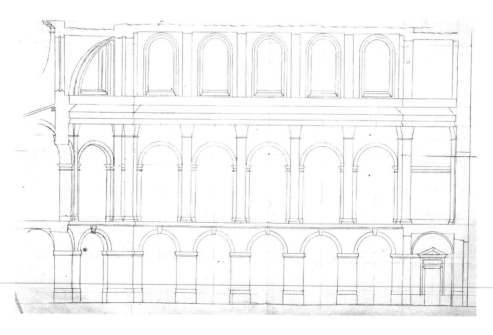

Figure 111. Office of Jules Hardouin-Mansart, Design for Versailles Chapel, Section. Drawing, 1688/9. Nationalmuseum, Stockholm. (Photo: Statens Konstmuseer.)

Figure 112. Office of Jules Hardouin-Mansart, Design for Versailles Chapel, Section. Drawing, 1698. Nationalmuseum, Stockholm. (Photo: Statens Konstmuseer.)

Figure 113. Jules Hardouin-Mansart, Versailles Chapel, Exterior, 1699–1710. (Photo: Author.)

Figure 114. Jules Hardouin-Mansart, Versailles Chapel, Interior, 1699–1710. (Photo: Archives Photographiques, Paris/S.P.A.D.E.M.)

Figure 115. Jules Hardouin-Mansart, Versailles Chapel, Vault, 1699–1710. (Photo: Archives Photographiques, Paris/S.P.A.D.E.M.)

Figure 116. Claude Perrault, Design for Sainte-Geneviève, Paris, Section. Drawing, 1670s. Bibliothèque Sainte-Geneviève, Paris. (Photo: Studio Ethel, Paris.)

Figure 117. Sainte-Chapelle, Paris, 1243–6. Exterior. (Photo: Archives Photographiques, Paris/S.P.A.D.E.M.)

Figure 118. Palatine Chapel, Aachen, ca. 796–805. Interior. (Photo: Bildarchiv Foto Marburg/Art Resource, New York.)

Construction continued smoothly despite a new conflict (the War of Spanish Succession, 1701–13); the painted and sculpted decorations were carried out from 1707 to 1710, in which year the chapel was dedicated. Mansart died during this campaign in 1708, and was replaced by Robert de Cotte, his brother-in-law, who also was promoted to first architect in that year.

The use of free-standing columns carrying a straight entablature was an innovation in French ecclesiastical architecture. This may reflect the influence of the Louvre Colonnade (Fig. 23), but Mansart may have known Claude Perrault's unpublished designs from the 1670s for the Parisian church of Sainte-Geneviève (Fig. 116), where this system was first proposed for a church. (The drawings, in the possession of Charles Perrault since Claude's death in 1688, had been given by Charles to the monks of Sainte-Geneviève in 1697, just before Mansart's revision of 1698/9.) The entablature and columns of the Versailles chapel are reinforced with iron to relieve the masonry of tensile stresses – the system of the Louvre Colonnade that Perrault also intended for his church.

Sculptural decoration of great profusion and variety was carried out by the leading royal sculptors. The spandrels of the nave (Fig. 114) were adorned with bas-reliefs depicting Christ's Passion, with prominent displays of the Instruments of the Passion – reminders of the Crown of Thorns, Nails, and part of the True Cross that had been purchased by Saint Louis from the Byzantine emperor in 1238 and received in Paris with great ceremony the next year. The vaults (Fig. 115) were painted in profuse Baroque style, with simulated revelations of the heavens and figures seen from below, the warm coloring contrasting with the brilliant whiteness of the stone and abundant light from the large, clear windows of the tribune level below. Louis XIV, seated with his family in the royal tribune, could gaze upon the mortals of the court gathered below and the heavenly spectacle painted above, where the Resurrection of Christ over the apse (Charles de La Fosse), God the Father in Paradise with Old Testament prophets over the nave (Antoine Coypel), and the Pentecost (Jean Jouvenet) overhead above his tribune could remind the King of his semidivine religious status, the anointed temporal intermediary between heaven and earth. Depictions of David, Constantine, Charlemagne, and Saint Louis, as well as abundant recurrences of royal French symbols like the fleur-de-lis and crossed L's (dual references to Louis IX and Louis XIV) proclaimed the chapel as the royal shrine of the Sun King, who could claim descent from these spiritual and dynastic ancestors. All of this imagery was harbored within a unique building that was simultaneously Gothic and contemporary in style and that thereby linked the third Bourbon with the French medieval past.

The Gothicism of the Versailles chapel is not an isolated phenomenon within the royal architecture. It will surely come as a surprise to learn that Claude Perrault regarded the Louvre Colonnade (Fig. 23) as harboring a Gothic quality, not in its forms – which are rigorously borrowed from the language of classical architecture – but in its spatial effects. The arrangement of paired columns creates intervals between the supports much wider than in customary practice. Perrault noted the fondness of the ancients for close columnar groupings. By contrast, he wrote (1673):

The taste of our century, or at least of our nation, is different from that of the ancients, and perhaps in that it owes a bit to the Gothic: because we like air, daylight, and openness. That has caused us to invent a sixth manner of placing columns, which is to join them two by two, and also to place the space of two intercolumniations in one. . . .

Rather than literally copy Gothic forms, Perrault, Mansart, and other French architects of the Louis XIV (and later) periods subtly used classical vocabulary and syntax to suggest Gothic spatial and aesthetic qualities. In the case of the Versailles chapel, the discerning viewer can detect Mansart's conscious intention; but the crypto-Gothicism of the Louvre façade can only be divined with the aid of Perrault's writings. That two of the most important royal structures of the reign partake of this medievalizing phenomenon is an indication of the seriousness with which Gothic architecture was beginning to be regarded, and offers a glimpse into the complexity of ideas that percolated in the minds of architects, patrons, and critics during the Ludovican age.

Before we leave Versailles at the end of the reign, some discussion is called for of the revolutionary developments in interior decoration that took place there and concurrently at the Château of Marly (Chap. 11). Although the King loved the outdoors – he was an avid horseman and hunter – the "craft of kingship," as he called it, necessitated many long hours within buildings, not to speak of his other activities, domestic and recreational. Like most of us, he was habitually surrounded by walls, ceilings, and floors that not only defined spatial volumes, but also exhibited types of finish and decoration. Ideas for Louis' domestic rooms were regularly submitted to him in the form of drawings whenever new work or the renovation of older interiors were undertaken. That is to say, the Sun King played a direct role in the formation of his intimate visual environment. The study of the royal domestic interiors is important for this reason, but even more so because it was in this arena of artistic activity that a revolutionary style was born – the Rococo – that was to have a development well into the eighteenth century that spread to all of Europe.

We have had a number of occasions to view some of the official, semipublic interiors at the Louvre and Versailles that were intended to impress the world (as they still do) with their splendor and magnificence. The Rococo decorative style, however, had its genesis in more intimate, domestic rooms designed for Louis XIV's personal use, and it is with interiors of this nature that we shall be concerned.

As a point of departure, let us examine two rooms in the Château of Versailles, dating from the central years of the reign. The marble paneling of the Salle des Gardes de la Reine (Hall of the Queen's Guards) (Fig. 119) originally decorated the King's Salon of Jupiter or Grand Cabinet, in which he would meet with his ministers, and dates from the 1670s. Marble was the most expensive of interior finishes, and was used in the Grand Cabinet because it formed part of the first Grand Appartement du Roi, sheathed entirely in that material. (Figure 55 shows another, more public room from that suite.)

The walls are scanned by rectangular frames in black marble, veined with white, that reach from floor to cornice. These frames enclose doors (with sculpted overdoors), the fireplace with its low overmantel and painting, another painting opposite, windows that overlook the garden, and a segment of wall facing these. We are struck by the heavy quality of the frames, which have pronounced projecting moldings. Areas of wall contained within the frames or between them receive bold geometric patterns (circles, losanges, rectangles, most with one curved side to accommodate the circles), all in mottled reddish-brown marble. Stripes of white marble form spaces between these geometric fields. The impression is one of rigidly geometrical shapes contained within an unyielding, massive armature. To the coloristic richness of black, white, and reddish-brown is added the gilt-stucco relief sculpture of the doors, overdoors, and swags framing the wall paintings. The white cornice also receives gilt-stucco ornament in the form of delicate, alternating motifs of shells and foliage connected by bands.

The walls, as eye-catching as they are, are really an overture to the main focus of the room, the painted coved ceiling divided into several framed pictures, the principal one in the center depicting Jupiter in a chariot pulled by eagles. In the corners of the room, between the accompanying paintings in the lower part of the cove with their massive frames, appear spectators looking down from parapets, with glimpses of sky beyond. This dominance of the painted vault is an Italian influence, and the entire room – designed under Le Brun's direction – may be called Baroque in style, entirely comparable to rooms decorated in seventeenth-century Italy.

For intimate rooms that were not directly linked within the *enfilade* of the Grands Appartements, much less expensive wooden paneling was more usual, as in the Cabinet du Billard of 1684 (Fig. 120). As in the earlier room, the walls are articulated by rectangular frames that enclose smaller geometric fields, in this case, all square or rectangular. A prominent over-

Figure 119. Salle des Gardes de la Reine, Château, Versailles, 1670s. (Photo: Réunion des Musées Nationaux.)

door with sculpted relief again appears (the circular frames between the eagles held still-life paintings), and now the chimneypiece is topped by a mirror, an innovation that was to receive later development. But the coved ceiling of this small room was simply painted white, like the wall panels, and this, too, foreshadowed later trends. The Cabinet du Billard was designed in Mansart's office, probably by one of his draftsmen called Lassurance.

Fifteen years later, in 1699, an apartment was arranged at Versailles for young Louis, Duc de Bourgogne, son of the Grand Dauphin; contemporary documents indicate that Louis XIV took close interest in this work. A drawing for the bedroom, by an unidentified draftsman in Mansart's bureau, is one of the incunabula of Rococo decorative style (Fig. 121). Here we find wood paneling as in the Cabinet du Billard, but with greater vertical unification. Very narrow unified strips, resembling pilasters, but without capitals and bases, run from the low dado to the cornice, and broader fields between them with central oval motifs recall the Grand Cabinet (Salle des Gardes de la Reine). But both narrow and broader panels are invaded by delicate, filigreelike foliate ornament in low carved relief, picked out in gold against the white paneling. Within the "pilasters," the motifs are contained within the rectangular frames, but in the broader sections, the ornament

Figure 120. Cabinet du Billard, Versailles, 1684. Engraving by Pierre Le Pautre. (Photo: from A. Marie and J. Marie, *Mansart à Versailles*, II, Paris, 1972.)

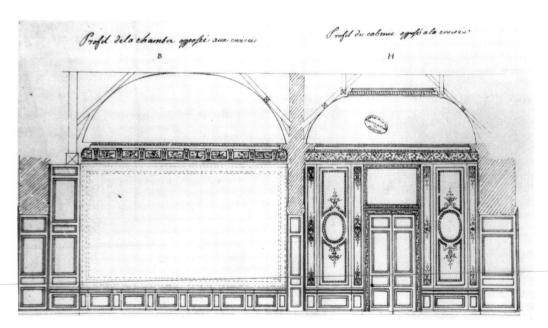

Figure 121. Office of Jules Hardouin-Mansart, Bedroom of the Apartment of the Duc de Bourgogne. Drawing, 1699. Archives Nationales, Paris. (Photo: from A. Marie and J. Marie, *Versailles au temps de Louis XIV*, Paris, 1976.)

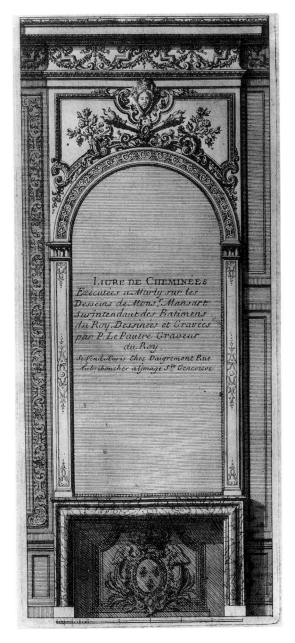

Figure 122. Pierre Le Pautre, Chimneypiece for Marly. Engraving, 1699. (Photo: The Metropolitan Museum of Art, New York, Harris Brisbane Dick Fund, 1933.)

Figure 123. Pierre Le Pautre, Rosette for King's Bedroom, Marly. Drawing, 1699. Bibliothèque Nationale, Paris, Cabinet des Estampes. (Photo: from F. Kimball, *The Creation of the Rococo,* Philadelphia, 1943.)

grows out of the curving frames that enclose the ovals and spreads into the empty enclosed fields. The traditional principle of a separation of frame and ornament is beginning to give way to a new idea in which the two are fused. This new decorative effect – seemingly trivial but with far-reaching consequences as realized in the subsequent history of art – has been attributed by the American architectural historian Fiske Kimball to Pierre Le Pautre, one of Mansart's draftsmen, who published a suite of engravings in that same year, 1699, showing his newly designed chimneypieces for Marly (Chap. 11; Fig. 122). These prints show the new type, with a simple low fireplace directly surmounted by a huge mirror within an arched frame (one of these mirrors can be seen in place on the upper floor of the King's Pavilion, Fig. 132, extreme left). The new delicate foliate decoration can be seen within the very slender pilasters, but it is above the mirror that the new decorative principle appears. In Figure 122, the lower corners of the frame above the arch turn into C-scrolls with characteristic hawks' bills and acanthus swirls. The straight top of the frame is transformed into looping scrolls to enclose a decorative face. Naturalistic sprigs of flowers grow out of the lower curved frames above the mirror to invade the blank, enclosed field.

Again at Marly in 1699, Le Pautre designed a prophetic ornamental rosette for the center of the ceiling of the King's bedroom; like most of the new decoration, which we call early Rococo, it was meant to be carved in wood in low relief. His drawing, which has survived (Fig. 123), shows the familiar radiant Apollo's head surrounded by circular frames, perhaps intended for paintings. The frames are enclosed within a field with no stable edge; the perimeter is defined by quirky, undulating, reverse-curve sprigs, and decorative growths sprout in all directions, poised to spread out over the blank white ceiling, as in later, mature Rococo examples.

Le Pautre brought the new mode to the Château of Versailles two years later in the Antichambre de l'Oeil-de-Boeuf (Fig. 124) – the room in the King's new personal suite of rooms where courtiers awaited entrance to the royal bedroom, where the ritualized *lever et coucher du roi* were enacted (the door at the right rear leads into the bedroom). We note the low fireplace with gracefully curved arch and high glass with concave upper corners in the spirit of the new Marly chimneypieces. In the right foreground, we have a view of one of the earliest large surviving panels of the early Rococo. The corners of the long rectangular field are concave with extremely intricate foliate arabesques; this decoration reappears, growing out of the end frames and central rosette, spreading horizontally over the empty field. We also see the decoration within the flanking, elongated pilasterlike strips. Again, the delicate, low relief carving is gilded, set off against the cream-white backgrounds.

Figure 124. Antichambre de l'Oeil-de-Boeuf, Versailles, 1701. (Photo: Lauros-Giraudon/Art Resource, New York.)

The ceiling of the Antichambre, also in cream white, is blank, but above the cornice appears an unusual decorated field, a sort of attic with a diagonal mosaic pattern. Against this field disport gilded nude children and youths in hedonistic abandon, with animals, flowers, and swags. It is tempting to see in these forms a direct reflection of the Kings' taste at the turn of the century. In 1699, in connection with proposed decoration for the apartment of the fourteen-year-old Duchesse de Bourgogne, arranged within one of the buildings of the Menagery of Versailles (Fig. 39), Louis wrote a famous note to Mansart:

It seems to me that some changes should be made, that the subjects are too serious, and that there should be some youthfulness mingled in what will be executed. You will bring me designs when you return, or at least some ideas. Childhood [or children] should be spread out everywhere [*Il faut de l'enfance répandue partout*].

Designs judged suitable for this mood were provided by Claude III Audran, an important decorator who worked under Mansart on this project. One of his surviving drawings for the ceiling of the Duchesse's apartment (1700) shows youthful figures intertwined with fantastic decorative motifs that suggest older modes of grotesque decoration. The imagery of childhood was then repeated in the Antichambre (Fig. 124) at Versailles the next year in conjunction with early Rococo decoration. The note to Mansart of 1699 would seem to be an indication of the Monarch's desire in his late years for a lighter, more delicate decorative mode associated with childhood and youth – a modulation in personal *goût* that encouraged the development of the Rococo, a style of infinite delicacy born within the royal works.

MARLY

The decision of early 1678 to create a splendid long gallery in the Château of Versailles (the future Galerie des Glaces; Fig. 96) was a signal that Versailles was soon to become the official seat of the Crown (officially proclaimed in 1682). That meant that the King's time there was going to be largely taken up with official business, receptions, and court etiquette; thus, a more informal abode where Louis could relax became a necessity. The other royal châteaux, all quite large, did not provide the appropriate ambiance, and the Porcelain Trianon at Versailles was too small, best suited for daytime visits only (Chap. 6; Fig. 56). In early 1679, the King personally visited potential sites in the neighborhood of Saint-Germain-en-Laye, searching for a setting where a pleasure dome might be built. He chose Marly, located halfway between Versailles and Saint-Germain. The air was considered better at Marly than at Versailles and there was an attractive view north to Saint-Germain. The commission was given to Hardouin-Mansart, probably soon after Le Nôtre's departure for Italy in the late winter of 1679. Mansart very quickly produced a total design for the buildings and the garden (Fig. 125); the scheme was approved and work began in the spring of 1679. The swampy ground was filled in and graded from south to north. The buildings started to rise in that year, and by 1684, the King's pavilion and its twelve small satellites were standing. Marly was shown in that year to members of the court and to the Algerian ambassador; in 1686, it was visited by the Siamese ambassadors and the King slept there for the first time. The garden and its decoration continued to evolve throughout the remainder of the reign.

This exquisite, unified creation was destroyed during the French Revolution and the early nineteenth century, the victim of antimonarchical fervor and capitalist greed. The general contours of the garden, however, still remain along with the entrance avenue, a few water basins, two statues, and

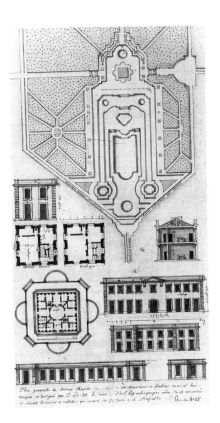

Figure 125. Office of Jules Hardouin-Mansart, Initial Design for Marly. Drawing, 1679. Nationalmuseum, Stockholm. (Photo: Statens Konstmuseer.)

the monumental horse trough at the north end. And thanks to remarkably rich visual documentation, the splendors of Marly can still be grasped (Figs. 126–8).

The originality and uniqueness of the design were noted in the *Mercure galant* in 1686, and modern architectural historians are still groping to identify the sources of Mansart's conception. Three features are immediately striking: the "decomposition" of the residential building into a principal unit and twelve subsidiaries; the integration of these buildings entirely *within* a garden; and the unusual number of water features found on the main axis, sloping from south to north.

The King's pavilion (Figs. 128, 129, 131, 132), elevated on a podium, immediately stood out as the main structure. It was a perfectly square, symmetrical building, with a plan evidently based on Palladio's Villa Rotonda (Fig. 130) – a very rare instance of Palladianism in French architecture that Fréart de Chambray had previously championed (Chap. 1). There are, to be sure, many changes: at Marly there are no porticoes with Roman temple stairs; the central vaulted two-story salon is octagonal, not round; the vestibules leading to the salon are much wider; and each corner suite contains more rooms. The ground floor at Marly was the principal one (as

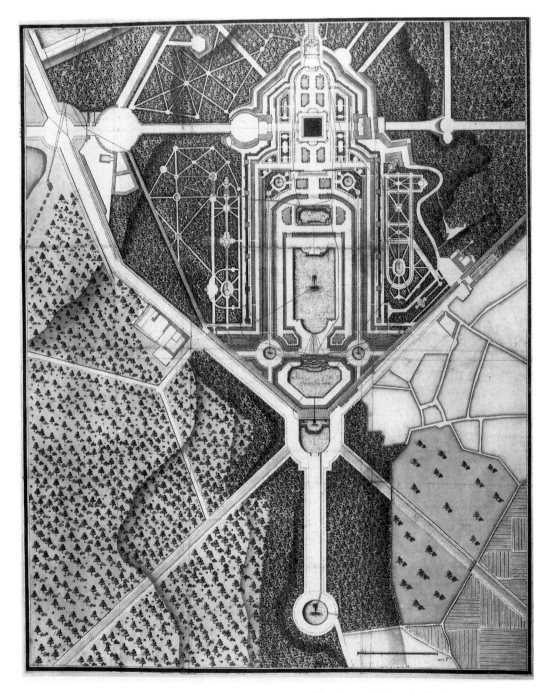

Figure 126. Marly, begun 1679. Final Plan. Drawing, Bibliothèque Nationale, Paris, Cabinet des Estampes. (Photo: Bibliothèque Nationale, Paris.)

in Palladio's building) and the suites were reserved for the King, the Grand Dauphin, Monsieur (Philippe d'Orléans, the King's brother), and Madame (Monsieur's second wife, Élisabeth-Charlotte von der Pfalz). Other members of the royal family could be lodged in smaller rooms on the upper floor, opening off an interior square corridor (Fig. 129, top). Each of the small pavilions (Fig. 128) had a three-room apartment on each of its two floors. These were for the favored guests whom Louis would invite to Marly. Such invitations were tokens of royal favor and were greatly prized. At Marly, the Sun King, casting aside his role as ruler of the kingdom, would assume a different *persona,* that of "first gentleman of France," indicated, for example, by allowing the courtiers to wear their hats in his presence when strolling in the garden. Such promenades were among a number of recreational activities at Marly, which included hunting in the neighboring forests, feasting, entertainments, and gambling in the salon of the King's pavilion, as well as several outdoor pastimes that look ahead to the modern country club and amusement park: the game of pall-mall (*le mail*), a swinging bucket that held several people, and a sled on rails (*la ramasse*) that sped down terrain – perhaps the earliest ancestor of the roller coaster (there was also a simpler version at Versailles).

These droll diversions did not, however, diminish the brilliance and subtlety of the artistic design. Returning to the King's pavilion and its exterior (Fig. 131), we note that the pitched roof over the coved vault of the central salon is nowhere in evidence; the upper part of the building is terminated by a pediment and balustrade with vases and sculpture, but without a visible roof, like the new Louvre façades (Figs. 23 and 27) and the Envelope of Versailles (Figs. 51 and 52). This roofless skyline was repeated in the twelve small pavilions, which were connected by iron trellises covered with climbing plants (Fig. 128). All the buildings (which were supplemented by a guardhouse, chapel, and service buildings with domestic quarters near the King's pavilion; Fig. 128) were cheaply built of brick-and-rubble masonry with ashlar quoins. The brick and rubble were covered with smooth plaster, in turn painted in fresco that simulated pilasters, balconies, and sculpture. This *trompe-l'oeil* decoration was designed by Le Brun and executed by his assistants at a moment (early 1680s) when Mansart and the first painter were also closely collaborating in the Galerie des Glaces and its salons at Versailles (Fig. 96). The polychromatic frescoes harmonized with the colorful flowers of the garden and helped to elucidate the iconographic program. The King's pavilion (painted with red "marble" Corinthian pilasters and gold "sculpture") was called the palace of the sun in the first extended description of Marly published in the *Mercure galant* in 1686; in each of its four pediments, Apollo appeared in his chariot, driving the horses of the sun at four different times of day, from daybreak to dusk (again, *trompe-l'oeil*

Figure 127. Pierre-Denis Martin, *View of Marly*, 1723. Musée National du Château de Versailles. (Photo: Réunion des Musées Nationaux.)

Figure 128. Detail of Fig. 127. (Photo: Réunion des Musées Nationaux.)

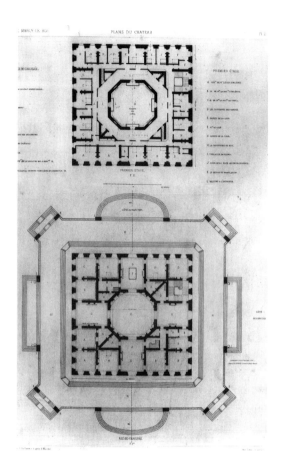

Figure 129. Jules Hardouin-Mansart, King's Pavilion, Marly, begun 1679. Plan of Ground Floor (bottom) and Upper Floor (top). Engraving from A. A. Guillaumot, *Château de Marly-le-Roi*, Paris, 1865. (Photo: Boston Public Library.)

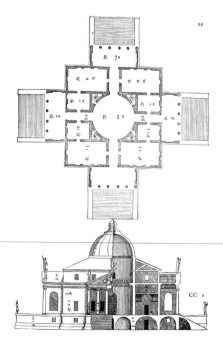

Figure 130. Andrea Palladio, Villa Rotonda, near Vicenza, 1550s. Plan, Elevation, and Section. Woodcut from A. Palladio, *I Quattro Libri dell'Architettura*, Venice, 1570. (Photo: Boston Public Library.)

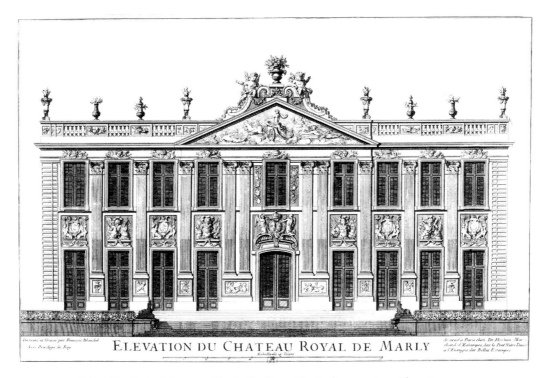

ELEVATION DU CHATEAU ROYAL DE MARLY

Figure 131. Jules Hardouin-Mansart, King's Pavilion, Marly, begun 1679. Elevation. Engraving by Jacques-François Blondel. (Photo: Bibliothèque Nationale, Paris.)

Figure 132. Jules Hardouin-Mansart, King's Pavilion, Marly, begun 1679. Section. Engraving from A. A. Guillaumot, *Château de Marly-le-Roi*, Paris, 1865. (Photo: Bibliothèque Nationale, Paris.)

paintings were used to simulate sculpture). After some early, iconographi-
cally complex ideas for the twelve small pavilions were proposed and rejected, they were alternatively painted (beginning in 1683) with red "marble" Ionic pilasters and gold balconies and busts, both types enriched with
gold trophies and reliefs (Fig. 128). The twelve pavilions were understood
to represent the signs of the zodiac, appropriately accompanying the palace
of the sun, the King's pavilion. Furthermore, the four royal suites of the
latter building (Fig. 129, bottom) alluded to the four seasons by overall
color scheme, and paintings of the seasons were placed in the central salon,
itself thought of as referring to the year by its octagonal plan, returning on
itself. In addition, the glitter of huge rock-crystal chandeliers throughout the
main house may have been intended to emphasize the solar iconography.

The basic arrangement of the main and twelve minor pavilions thus
continued the pervasive Apollonian imagery of Louis XIV's entire reign, but
another classical idea was in the minds of court intellectuals and perhaps in
those of the King and his architect as well: Louis' Marly as the modern
counterpart to Augustus's villas, to which that emperor repaired for repose.
We know that in 1692, Jean Racine and Nicolas Boileau, distinguished
members of the Petite Académie (Chap. 3), proposed a medal (not struck)
showing Marly with the motto RECESSVI NON OTIO, translated by Racine
and Boileau as "For being more solitary but not for ceasing to act." These
writers explained that

Augustus, crowned with glory, and burdened with the cares of the empire of the
world, finding himself at times annoyed by the tumult of the court and by the
crowd of courtiers, had chosen places outside of Rome in order to collect his
thoughts and rest a bit. LANUVIUM, PRAENESTE, TIBUR were his usual retreats. The
letter that that emperor wrote to the Senate on this subject shows how much he
believed that solitude was useful from time to time in order to reflect on his
administration and to gather new strength.

This is what gave the idea for this architectural medal. . . . This year Marly is
designated as the place where the King takes his pleasure and retires from his Court.

Solitude was not exactly what Louis sought at Marly, but rather a more
relaxed atmosphere where he could be accompanied by a relatively small
group of *invités*. In all other respects, however, Marly was to function like
Augustus's villas (and like Versailles itself during the 1660s and most of
the 1670s).

The small pavilions flanked the central part of the garden, composed of
terraces of earth, separated by slopes of grass (Figs. 126–8). These pavilions
stood on the outermost, highest terrace, remarkable for its trees shaped into
the form of groin vaults – delicate, fragile canopies on slender trunks. The
terraces suggested rows of tiers in a theater from which to observe the

Figure 133. André Le Nôtre(?), La Rivière, Marly, 1697–8. Engraving by Jacques Rigaud. (Photo: Bibliothèque Nationale, Paris.)

spectacular series of hydraulic features that defined the main (south to north) axis of the garden. The Machine of Marly (1681–4; Chap. 10) assured a plentiful supply of water, pumped up from the Seine into huge reservoirs. The water first emerged on the central axis at the south in the form of an unusually long step cascade called La Rivière (the River, 200 meters long with 52 steps; Fig. 133). This was the one feature at Marly probably due to Le Nôtre, but not built until 1697–8, and hence not part of Mansart's original scheme. After flowing into a still-extant basin at the foot of the cascade, the waters reemerged to the north of the King's pavilion in a rectangular basin with four vertical jets; then they appeared again in the Grand Miroir (Great Mirror), a basin of complex shape with five jets, with a long axis that stressed the main garden axis; finally, the waters flowed over low cascades of complex, graceful curves into a wedge-shaped basin at the north. Below the northern end wall at the level of the town, a public horse trough was built with an upper display basin with three jets (1698–9; Fig. 128). The garden axis continued toward the north, terminated by a round basin with a high jet (Fig. 126).

It was at this still-extant northern edge of the garden that two marble horse-and-rider groups were put in place in 1702. These groups of *Fame* and *Mercury* (Figs. 127 and 128) (commissioned in 1698 and carved in 1701–2 by Antoine Coysevox; now in Paris, Tuileries Garden) are allegories celebrating the fame of Louis XIV in war (*Fame*) and peace (*Mercury*), and although turned inward to face the garden, they were also visible on their high pedestals from the town roads; hence, these sculptures were the only features of this private royal residence visible to the outer world. The theme

Figure 134. Nicolas Bertin(?), *Allegory of Louis XIV at Marly.* Drawing, Bibliothèque Nationale, Paris, Cabinet des Estampes. (Photo: Bibliothèque Nationale, Paris.)

of the King's warlike deeds was echoed in the main pavilion, with its simulated exterior trophies (Fig. 131) and its interiors (Fig. 132) hung with paintings of battles and sieges by Van der Meulen. The theme of Louis XIV as the bringer of peace (the War of the League of Augsburg had ended in 1697) was celebrated by the garden of Marly itself, as is attested by a poem (1697) by François Boutard and by an allegorical drawing (Fig. 134) in which Louis, seated on a cloud, turns away from armed Minerva to accept the caduceus of peace, accompanied by images of abundance and fertility. Below, putti-gardeners go about their work in front of La Rivière.

During the last fifteen years of the reign (ca. 1700–15), sculpture was distributed throughout the garden, representing nature deities and pastoral/hunting themes. The emphasis shifted from the Sun King to the "genius of the place," and the sculptures celebrated Marly as a country retreat. Many of these sculptures were placed in *bosquets* developed (from 1687/8 on) behind the ranges of small pavilions (Figs. 127 and 128). Here could be found fountains and garden features of great variety. In contrast to Versailles and most earlier French gardens, the *bosquets* were linked by avenues, allowing glimpses from one *bosquet* into another – a feature presaging later eighteenth-century garden developments.

In 1686, the *Mercure galant* characterized the exterior frescoes of Marly

(Figs. 128 and 131) as "à la manière d'Italie" (in Italian style). We have already noted the dependence of the plan of the King's pavilion on Palladio's Villa Rotonda. It should be added at this point that the relationship of La Rivière (Fig. 133) to the main building is reminiscent of the Villa Aldobrandini, Frascati, which Le Nôtre may have visited in 1679. (A drawing from Le Nôtre's studio of 1685 shows a first idea for the Marly cascade; his cousin, Michel Le Bouteux, made designs in 1680 of ideal gardens with cascades axially aligned on the main house.)

Marly therefore may be said to have been the most Italianate of Louis XIV's residences. Yet its Italian sources were transfigured into a masterpiece of great originality and fastidious refinement. Because Marly no longer exists, we cannot directly experience its aesthetic spell, but must rely on voices from the past. In 1774, Jacques-François Blondel, an architect and a great connoisseur of French architecture, wrote:

The end of day would lead to a new enchantment. When nature's rest brings on the reign of silence, I would invite you to admire the situation of the surroundings. You would see how much their picturesque look serves to highlight the studied symmetry of these gardens, the beautiful effect of their waters, and the almost magical linkage of architecture, sculpture, and the art of gardening; objects united here by taste and genius (*L'homme du monde éclairé par les arts*).

The "surroundings" that Blondel mentions in this passage probably included the forests visible to the east, west, and south beyond the garden (Figs. 126 and 127). To the north, the deep vista over the Seine to Saint-Germain-en-Laye was a very narrow one, defined by the opening of trees flanking the terminal avenue and round basin at the north end of the composition (Fig. 126). True to the tradition of the French formal garden, Mansart kept the visitor's main focus on the man-made composition, with its "objects united . . . by taste and genius."

PARIS – II

Beginning in the 1680s, royal squares (*places royales*) started to appear in Paris and in a few provincial towns. The *place royale* was a square built around a statue of the King as its focus. Surrounded by uniform façades, the *place* provided welcome open space within usually congested urban fabrics. Urban squares had existed in France at least since the time of Henry IV, and his aristocratic, residential Place Royale in Paris (now Place des Vosges), dating from 1605–12 (Fig. 135), with its equestrian statue of Louis XIII at the center of the space, was an important predecessor of the later *places*. But the Place Royale had not been designed from the outset around the ruler image (the statue was erected in 1639), and its brick-and-stone architecture with shops and clumsy Doric pilasters at ground level was considered insufficiently dignified in the eyes of the Sun King and his contemporaries. The innovative and influential Parisian *places royales* created under Louis XIV were not envisaged on the Blondel-Bullet map of 1675–6 (Fig. 64), but were developed from the 1680s on. They took their *raison d'être* from their statues of the King, and their surrounding architecture thus had to be somehow appropriate in both form and function to the central monarchic images; alternatives would have to be found to the elevations of the old Place Royale and the other squares of Henry IV's architects.

The *places royales* were usually the initiatives of private individuals or of municipalities, not of the Crown. But the climate for their creation was fostered by the King, who encouraged panegyric gestures, and by the optimistic temper of the 1680s, when France was basking in a short-lived peace following the successful conclusion of the Dutch War in 1678. Yet, in a few instances, the Crown founded the square, as in the first phase of the Place Louis-le-Grand (Vendôme) in Paris, discussed in what follows.

Between 1684 and 1688 there were seventeen proposals in sixteen cities for *places royales*, but few were realized, mainly because of municipal funding problems. The two main provincial squares from the Louis XIV period that survive are in Dijon (now Place de la Libération) and Lyon (now Place Bellecour). The first was begun in 1685 under Mansart, but the complex history of the Place Bellecour extends from 1659 to 1726, with both Mansart and his successor, Robert de Cotte, playing important roles (a royal statue for the Lyon square was first proposed in 1685). But neither *place* is particularly distinguished, and they need not detain us from proceeding to examine the important Parisian examples.

The first in the series is the Place des Victoires in Paris (Figs. 136 and 137), due to a loyal and grateful aristocrat, the Maréchal de La Feuillade. In 1682, La Feuillade signed a contract with the sculptor Martin Desjardins for a bronze statue of Louis XIV to be displayed in a public square. The Maréchal purchased the necessary land, obtained permission from the municipality to create a *place* (funded by himself), and engaged the first architect, Hardouin-Mansart, in 1685 to design it. Desjardin's statue, installed in November of that year, was dedicated in March 1686 with members of the royal family present (the King, ill, could not attend). La Feuillade, on horseback, rode around the square three times with his regiment; fireworks were set off in the evening, and printed descriptions of the statue along with commemorative medals were distributed. The surrounding buildings – private *hôtels* without shops – were erected from 1687 to 1690.

The Place des Victoires – named in honor of the King's military triumphs – was thus a residential square, located to the north of the Louvre and at a convenient distance from it. It was laid out as a circle, flattened on one side by a straight street and two older *hôtels* that La Feuillade was unable to purchase (visible in Fig. 136). Five streets entered the *place*, thus creating an open square, which allowed views of the statue and glimpses of its architecture from the outside. Traffic was meant to flow through it, yet it provided welcome open space within Paris's otherwise dense urban network.

The façades defining a *place royale* had to be consonant with royal dignity. Mansart designed an arcaded ground floor of smoothly channeled masonry with keystone masks. Above this is the main floor, the *premier étage*, with tall rectangular windows topped with lintels on slender brackets; the *deuxième étage* above, somewhat lower in height, has simple rectangular window frames. Both upper floors are tied together by a colossal Ionic pilaster order with full entablature. The visible French roof is broken by dormer windows of alternating shape. The vertical edges of each block of buildings are defined by uniform quoins, with a slight inflection of the entablature. We may imagine the ground floor (textured, without a classical order) used for service areas, storage, and servants' quarters, the two upper floors (defined by the pilasters) for the owner and his family, and more

Figure 135. Place Royale (des Vosges), Paris, 1605–12. Engraving by Perelle. (Photo: Bibliothèque Nationale, Paris.)

servants under the roof. In 1689, the King's Council ordered the owners of the houses that La Feuillade was unable to buy to harmonize their façades with those of the *place*.

Mansart's elevation was directly derived from the Hôtel de Lully (Fig. 138), only a few streets away, built for the composer Jean-Baptiste Lully in 1671 by Daniel Gittard. Once again, as at the Invalides, we find the younger Mansart directly dependent on another architect's design. The elevation of Lully's house and those of the Place des Victoires were derived from the prestigious new south façade of the Louvre, begun in 1668 (Chap. 4; Fig. 27). The Place des Victoires proved to be a very influential prototype for the *places royales* of the later seventeenth and eighteenth centuries; because of their pedigree, its façades must have been perceived as suitable for royal imagery, a worthy setting for the focal object, Desjardin's statue of the Sun King, set in the center of the space with a railing around it. This gilt bronze statue (destroyed, like all royal statues in public locations, during the French Revolution) portrayed the Sun King in a standing pose, dressed in his coronation robes. As he stepped on the head of Cerberus (a symbol of religious heresy), a figure of Victory, perched behind him on a globe and holding a palm branch, crowned him with a laurel wreath. At the base of the tall pedestal upon which this group stood were four chained slaves, representing defeated nations (now in the park of Sceaux, south of Paris). Important features of the *place* were columnar lampposts around the periph-

Figure 136. Jules Hardouin-Mansart, Place des Victoires, Paris, 1685–90. View. Engraving from C. F. Menestrier, *Histoire du roy Louis le Grand, par les médailles . . .*, new ed., Paris, 1691. (Photo: Houghton Library, Harvard University.)

Figure 137. Jules Hardouin-Mansart, Place des Victoires, Paris, 1685–90. (Photo: Author.)

Figure 138. Daniel Gittard, Hôtel de Lully, Paris, 1671. (Photo: Author.)

ery, topped with large ships' lanterns that were lit at night (only two lampposts – much larger and more elaborate than those installed since 1667 in the streets of Paris – were erected). The lanterns imparted the aura of a holy shrine to the *place,* and a contemporary book on sculptural monuments linked the feature to classical antiquity by stating that the ancients had used lighting for honorific statues. It should be noted, however, that in 1699, Louis XIV discontinued the special illumination, feeling that such lamps were suitable only for churches. This gesture of the King was consonant with his later religiosity that developed from the 1680s on under the influence of Madame de Maintenon and that found its fullest expression in the final chapel at Versailles (Chap. 10).

The Maréchal de La Feuillade was aided in his enterprise by his friend, the Marquis de Louvois, who had succeeded Colbert in 1683 as superintendent of the King's buildings. Louvois was also an important player in the history of the next Parisian *place royale,* the Place Louis-le-Grand, today known as the Place Vendôme. In 1685, Louvois, representing the Crown, signed a contract with the Duc de Vendôme and the Capuchin fathers, who owned property on the Right Bank to the north of the Tuileries gardens. The contract called for the sale of their property to the Crown for the creation of a *place royale.* Later that year (1685, the year in which Hardouin-Mansart designed the Place des Victoires), he devised a rectangular plan for the new site, which was to be rimmed with government buildings: the royal library, academies, mint, and residence for extraordinary ambassadors. A print of this scheme was made (Fig. 139), showing uniform elevations around three sides, with the fourth (south) side open to the Rue Saint-Honoré and the monastery of the Feuillants. The elevation was very similar to that of the Place des Victoires, except that an arcaded portico (reminiscent of the Place Royale [des Vosges] in Paris; Fig. 135) ran all around the *place* at ground-floor level, and the windows of the main floor were distinguished by pediments. An entrance at the north end in the form of a triumphal arch, allowing a view of the new church of the Capucines, was to close the space. In the center was projected a huge bronze equestrian statue of the King dressed as a Roman emperor, his horse in a walking pose, the group placed upon a tall pedestal. The commission for this work was given to François Girardon.

This ambitious program for a governmental square was modified the very next year (1686) when it was realized that the buildings would produce no income for the royal treasury. Although Louvois still insisted on the creation of a royal library on the west side of the square, the King's Council decreed that elsewhere the Crown would erect *only façades* around the *place*; the land behind them would then be sold to private individuals who could build their houses behind the uniform fronts. Construction of the foundations began that same year. (Figure 139 actually shows the *place* with only the façades erected.) The scheme guaranteed uniform exteriors behind which could appear a diversity of plans – the same principle that governed the Place des Victoires and, before that, the Place Royale (des Vosges).

A contract for the royal library was issued in 1691, but later that year Louvois died and all work was halted by the King. France was now in the midst of the costly War of the League of Augsburg (1688–97), which saw the temporary suspension of much royal building activity, including the chapel of Versailles (Chap. 10). With the return of peace in 1698, the decision was made to omit the library, and at the end of that year or early in 1699, Louis XIV washed his hands of the project. He ceded the property to the city of Paris (except for a parcel reserved for his first architect, who in the same year was additionally elevated to the post of superintendent of the King's buildings), and the municipality was to construct the *place* according to a new design by Mansart. The plots of land were to be sold by the city to private parties for residential *hôtels*. Mansart submitted plans in 1699, and in August of that year, Girardon's great equestrian statue and pedestal were uncovered and dedicated in an impressive ceremony. The officials and militia of Paris, mounted and on foot, assembled in a great cortege that moved from the Hôtel de Ville (town hall) to the *place*. The statue was uncovered to cries of "Vive le Roi," and the *Mercure galant* reported that the members of the procession saluted the statue with "une profonde inclination." The ceremony was witnessed by a huge throng, to whom money was distributed. One of the Latin inscriptions on the pedestal honored the Monarch as an embellisher of Paris. Fireworks followed that evening, along with the spectacle of a temporary "Temple of Glory," erected on the Seine, with a "copy" of the statue glorified within.

Veüe et perspectiue de la place de Louis le Grand
fait par Aueline Auec Priuilege du Roy

Figure 139. Jules Hardouin-Mansart, First Project, Place Louis-le-Grand, Paris, 1685. Engraving by Pierre Aveline. (Photo: Bibliothèque Nationale, Paris.)

The square, now called Place Louis-le-Grand, was still surrounded by the façades of the first scheme. But demolition of these began the next month (September 1699), and Mansart's revised design of that year went into effect (Fig. 140). Instead of a rectangle, the plan of the *place* was now an irregular octagon: *hôtels* could be built behind the beveled corners, something not possible in a plan with right angles. Buyers could purchase from two to ten bays of façade and build a *hôtel* behind of any plan whatever. Unlike the Place des Victoires, the new square was basically of the closed type, with openings only on the north and south sides framing views of church façades. The Place Louis-le-Grand was thus not integrated into existing street patterns, as was the Place des Victoires, but was an isolated residential island within a developing part of the city.

Its new façade elevations (largely complete by September 1701; Fig. 141) followed the basic scheme of the Place des Victoires: a ground floor smoothly rusticated with a blind arcade (no portico), serving as a pedestal for the two upper floors, united by an order of colossal Corinthian pilasters, with dormers of alternating shape in the high roof. At the sides of the *place* and at the beveled corners, *avant-corps* appear with engaged columns subsumed under pediments. Symbols of the Sun King (radiant Apollo heads,

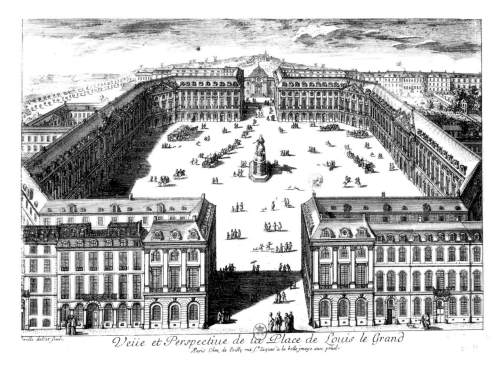

Figure 140. Jules Hardouin-Mansart, Place Louis-le-Grand (Vendôme), Paris, begun 1699. Engraving by Perelle. (Photo: Bibliothèque Nationale, Paris.)

Figure 141. Jules Hardouin-Mansart, Place Louis-le-Grand (Vendôme), Paris, begun 1699. (Photo: Author.)

crowned L's, etc.) could be found in the pediments, the ironwork railings, and on the streetlights (a by-now common feature of Paris), and all was dominated by Girardon's commanding statue. The variety of *hôtel* plans eventually developed behind the uniform façades was much greater than at earlier Parisian squares, due to the bevelled corners of the *place,* the greater elaborateness of the houses, and the increased sophistication of the architects.

Both the Place des Victoires and the Place Louis-le-Grand attracted not the aristocracy but a group of *nouveaux riches* financiers. Their flocking to these new residential areas, particularly to the latter, was a harbinger of the later urban history of Paris, which witnessed an accelerated development of the western part of the Right Bank. The corresponding part of the Left Bank, the area of the Faubourg Saint-Germain, was already experiencing great growth under Louis' reign, but its inhabitants were drawn mainly from the aristocracy. These developments on both banks were influenced by the great magnet of Versailles, lying to the southwest.

VAUBAN AND THE
ARCHITECTURE OF WAR

From his deathbed in 1715, the seventy-seven-year-old Louis XIV advised his five-year-old successor (later Louis XV): "Try to remain at peace with your neighbors. I loved war too much. Do not follow me in that. . . ."

Indeed, war had been an almost constant accompaniment of the reign. And the King directly experienced the front, both under the tutelage of Mazarin in his adolescence and in his maturity as an active commander. He still oversaw sieges as late as the 1690s during the War of the League of Augsburg, and Rigaud's portrait of 1694 (Fig. 142) was meant to give assurance that Louis cut as dashing a figure on the field of Mars during those years as he did in his youth.

The bellicose foreign policy of the Sun King necessitated a large defense budget for the erection of inland and coastal military structures that protected the borders and shores of France. For most of the reign, these constructions were designed and built under the supervision of Sébastien Le Prestre, Marquis de Vauban (1633–1707), a soldier and military engineer who became the greatest siege-warfare expert of his age.

This is not the place to rehearse the principles and practice of war during the Old Regime. But it should at least be understood that land warfare mainly consisted in the establishment or seizure of fortified positions, situated at strategic topographical points. Within these strongholds, a force of men could live and venture forth to control an area. If attacked, the fortification would hopefully shelter and protect the garrison long enough until a rescuing army arrived to lift the siege. It was always understood that, given sufficient time, any fortress would eventually fall to the attacker, if only because the defenders would exhaust their food and water supplies. The attempt of the attackers to capture the fortified position (much of it proceeding by the digging of trenches) and its defense by the armed inhabitants constituted the science of siege warfare.

Figure 142. Hyacinthe Rigaud, *Louis XIV*, 1694. Prado, Madrid. (Photo: MAS.)

During the Louis XIV period, this type of warfare was conducted according to remarkably systematic and codified tactics. Because the general nature of all fortifications was known, and because the available military technology (gunpowder, cannons, muskets) was stable and not subject to rapid and surprising innovation, siege operations proceeded in a standardized sequence; Vauban himself calculated that a successful siege would generally last forty-eight days, and it was not difficult to calculate approximately what the attacker would be up to on any given day. The capitulation of a fortress was a ritualized event: some of the defeated defenders marched out with bullets clenched in their teeth (to suggest that the soldiers were still militarily potent), with others singing or playing the martial music of the conqueror (a compliment). The civil representatives of the fortification (which usually contained a town) presented the besiegers with the city keys as well as with bread and salt (ancient symbols of submission).

Vauban emerged as a royal military engineer in 1667 when he was requested by the war minister, the Marquis de Louvois, to present a counter-project for the citadel of Lille, a northern city captured from the Spanish in that year. After receiving Vauban's proposal (a drawing, probably accompanied by a written explication), Louvois showed it to the King who discussed it with him and other advisers. The scheme was accepted, but Louvois' letter to Vauban records some technical changes and reveals Louis' very close attention to the details of fortification. The next year, Vauban was named governor and the enormous citadel was begun (building continued until 1693).

When at the front, Louis XIV had the opportunity to personally inspect the works, and a letter of 1687 by the great dramatist and royal historiographer Jean Racine reported the King's animal enthusiasm when exploring the defenses of the city of Luxembourg:

The truth apparently is that the King has taken relish in his conquest, and he is not displeased to examine it entirely at leisure. He has already viewed all the fortifications one after the other, has entered as far as the counter-mines of the covered way, which are very beautiful, and especially has been very pleased to see those famous redoubts between the two covered ways that gave Monsieur de Vauban so much trouble. Today the King is going to examine the circumvallation, that is, make a tour of seven or eight leagues.

Further indication of the regular involvement of Louis XIV in his fortifications is indicated by a diary entry (1694) by the Marquis de Dangeau: "The King does not go out after dinner; he works with Monsieur Le Peletier [de Souzy, the director-general of fortifications] . . . as he is in the habit of doing every Monday."

Beginning in 1668, the Monarch had yet another way of studying his fortifications. In that year, upon the suggestion of Louvois, the first of a series of three-dimensional models, or *plans-reliefs,* was fabricated of a fortified town. Built for the most part to the uniform scale of 1:600, these remarkably detailed confections of wood, displayed on tables, allowed the King to view, as if from a mountain top, his fortified cities and strongholds, laid out with amazing accuracy (Figs. 143 and 146). By 1697, 144 *plans-reliefs* depicting 108 different sites had been built, stocked in the Tuileries Palace and, during the last years of the reign, progressively displayed in the Grande Galerie connecting the Louvre and Tuileries. (Louis XIV generally examined them before they were sent to Paris.) Guarded as state military secrets, the *plans-reliefs* could be viewed only with royal permission. That explains why there are no contemporary depictions of the models. Although such maquettes had on occasion been created in other countries (Italy and

Figure 143. Belfort, *Plan-Relief.* Musée de l'Armée, Hôtel des Invalides, Paris. (Photo: Archives Photographiques, Paris/S.P.A.D.E.M.)

Figure 144. Belfort, View of Entrance to City, after 1687. (Photo: Author.)

Figure 145. Besançon, View of Entrance to Citadel, from 1678. (Photo: Author.)

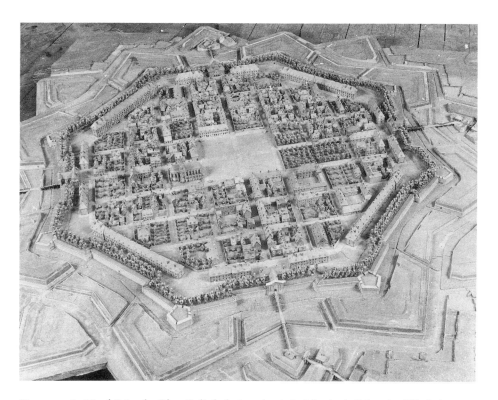

Figure 146. Neuf-Brisach, *Plan-Relief*, designed 1698. Musée de l'Armée, Hôtel des Invalides, Paris. (Photo: Archives Photographiques, Paris/S.P.A.D.E.M.)

Germany) since the first half of the sixteenth century, the French initiative was new in its accuracy, encyclopedic scope, and rigorous usage in military planning.

Vauban, in a letter of 1695 written from Brest, suggested to Le Peletier that they view the *plan-relief* of Namur together: "I will have you touch, by finger and eye, all the defects of that fortress, which are considerable, and at the same time have you perceive in what way the one that is imputed to me can be corrected; and you will see that it can only be corrected with great expenditure of time and money." A visit to the site itself was unnecessary; the model in Paris would suffice for discussions between the director–general and his military engineer.

The walls, bastions, ditches, and outer defensive elements of Louis XIV's fortifications – often huge in scale – still exist in considerable numbers, and anyone who explores them today cannot but be impressed by the enormous amount of money and labor that must have gone into their creation. In a view of the entrance side of Belfort (Franche-Comté) – a city with older fortifications that Vauban reworked after 1687 (Fig. 144; cf. foreground of Fig. 143) – we see the high town wall extending back from the right edge of the illustration into the center background. The city gate (under restoration in Fig. 144) punctuates the expanse of wall. Extending before the walls is a huge ditch, traversed by a bridge leading to the gate. This critical access to the town entrance is in turn protected by a separate defensive segment or outwork, manned by soldiers, with its own small portal (left middle distance). Its walls are lower than those of the town, so that if an enemy captured the outwork, the town defenders would retain the advantage of higher ground for their artillery and muskets. Even after capturing the outwork, the attackers would then be faced with the ultimate formidable task of crossing the ditch, raked by withering cross-fire. A similar system can be seen at the entrance to the citadel of Besançon (Franche-Comté) (reworked from 1678 on; Fig. 145), where the fortifications grow out of exposed natural rock, adding to the impression of indestructibility.

Belfort and Besançon show the Sun King's fortifications on a colossal scale. Much smaller but illustrative of the mature perfection of Vauban's final ideas is one of his last undertakings – the newly created garrison town of Neuf-Brisach (Alsace), a watch on the Rhine (designed 1698, built 1699–1712). Vauban's third and final project was sent to Louis XIV in 1698 at Versailles, and Le Peletier wrote back to the royal engineer, reporting that "I saw the project for it [Neuf-Brisach] yesterday in the hands of the King, which I can assure you he began to look over at nine-thirty in the evening." Royal approval followed. Working *ex nihilo*, Vauban designed the town as an octagon with a checkerboard pattern of blocks and streets accommodated within (Fig. 146). Although he had used a radial pattern of avenues (favored by Italian Renaissance theory and practice) in the early pentagonal citadel at Lille (Fig. 153) — perhaps as a reference to royal solar imagery (sculpted radiant suns appear on the vaulted passageways within the Porte Royale, Fig. 150) — Vauban in his later schemes favored a checkerboard, resulting in a square (as at Neuf-Brisach) or rectangular *place d'armes* in the center of the town. At Neuf-Brisach, as in his other urban creations, the town square is bordered by important public buildings (houses for the governor and high officers, church, town hall), and it was here that the entire garrison would assemble. Most of the blocks were taken up with houses, shops, and market buildings for the civilian population, with a few military structures interspersed (arsenal, storage depots, military hospital). Along the periphery of the octagon were placed long buildings with end pavilions — the barracks for the troops and officers (Fig. 147). All of this — the town proper — was contained within curtain walls with recessed central ranges and projecting bastions, built at a sloped angle to best resist cannon bombardment (Fig. 148). Set within the walls and bastions were enclosed, specially ventilated chambers (casemates) for artillery pieces that could fire upon attackers who had managed to reach the curtain wall. Placed in front of the curtain wall all around the fortress was a complex system of detached outworks in the form of wedge-shaped units. Entrance into the town was provided by bridges leading to four gateways on opposite sides of the octagon, each gate (Fig. 149) protected by a special outwork with an obtuse angle. The land around Neuf-Brisach was formed into a clearing, sloping away from the town (the *glacis*), so that approaching troops could be clearly seen and exposed to defensive fire.

Vauban was primarily concerned with the efficiency of the fortification under the stress of war, the disposition of its walls, ditches, and outer defenses, and the general arrangement of the buildings and arteries within. But he also was responsible for the design of individual features and buildings, and in this he was assisted by a staff of draftsmen, comparable to that provided the first architect. In a letter to Louvois from Strasbourg (1681), he wrote of "three draftsmen [who] have worked incessantly since your departure and . . . , as for myself, I have only come and gone, written, corrected, and adjusted their work." The actual construction was left to local architects and masons, using local materials, and this accounts to some extent for the wide variety of style in Vauban's constructions, strewn all around the perimeter of France.

However, in his first work, the citadel of Lille (begun 1668), Vauban relied on local masons who had worked under Spanish rule until the French conquest. The main entrance to the citadel, the Porte Royale (Fig. 150), was designed unimaginatively on the model of a church façade with scroll-volutes connecting the two stories. The exterior face of the secondary en-

Figure 147. Neuf-Brisach, Barracks, 1699–1712. (Photo: Author.)

trance, the Porte Dauphine (Fig. 151), is more original, with overlapping wall planes and a broad segmental pediment that unifies the entire portal. A lyre next to the radiant Apollo's head in the pediment, amidst the obligatory imagery of war, unexpectedly reminds us of the King's contributions to the arts. One detects a Flemish profuseness and complexity in these gates, foreign to the French aesthetic. Later portals are also very varied, but reveal a more consistent Gallic sensibility. At Longwy (Lorraine), the Porte de France (after 1678; Fig. 152) displays a smoothly rusticated enframement around the recessed opening (a motif lifted from contemporary French domestic or civic architecture; note the roof) framed by decorated piers topped with military trophies (suggestive of garden gates) – a somewhat uneasy coupling of disparate forms. In a gateway from Neuf-Brisach (Fig. 149), a flat, pilastered temple-front portico appears, set against a recessed wall with end pilasters, the whole unified by a continuous entablature and horizontal banding to suggest robustness. This late composition, modest as it is, returns us to a vocabulary closer to the royal works (cf. Figs. 27 and 131), and therefore it comes as little surprise to learn that the design was provided by the office of the first architect, Mansart – a departure from the usual pattern of Vauban using his own group of designers. But the structures at Neuf-Brisach were built by a local entrepreneur using local materials.

Other individual buildings erected under Vauban within the towns and citadels include barracks (Fig. 153), arsenals (Fig. 154), governors' houses (Fig. 155), and chapels, to name some of the more important types. The

Figure 148. Neuf-Brisach, Fortifications, 1699–1712. (Photo: Author.)

Figure 149. Neuf-Brisach, Porte de Colmar, 1699–1712. (Photo: Author.)

Figure 150. Citadel, Lille, Porte Royale, after 1668. (Photo: Author.)

Figure 151. Citadel, Lille, Porte Dauphine, after 1668. (Photo: Author.)

Figure 152. Longwy, Porte de France, after 1678. (Photo: Author.)

chapels, like the gates, come in an assortment of styles. The Lille chapel (Fig. 153) – a simple rectangular hall with an apsidal end – received a familiar, two-story pilastered screen with scroll volutes, reminiscent of the Porte Royale there (Fig. 150). Later, at the citadel of Besançon in Franche-Comté, a chapel of radically simplified form was built (consecrated in 1683; Fig. 156). Whereas the Lille façade strongly recalls older (specifically sixteenth-century) architecture and could suggest an interior space with nave and side aisles (there is only a single hall), the Besançon design is much less derivative and states the single-space interior unequivocally on the exterior. Decorative touches are reduced, classical pilasters appear only around the small portal, and huge side windows flood the interior with light. One is tempted to describe the later work as more "functional" in appearance, and it anticipates the aesthetic of French architecture of a century later.

Sometimes Vauban and his assistants devised buildings with interesting structural features. A case in point is the powder magazine, built to a standardized design. The well-preserved example in the Lille citadel (Fig. 157) shows the unusual number of pier buttresses – borrowed from medieval architecture – bracing the rectangular building on all sides to withstand the force of an explosion. The magazine itself is recessed in an excavated area surrounded by a wall to further isolate it. The casks of powder were

Figure 153. Citadel, Lille, View of Place d'Armes and Chapel, after 1668. (Photo: Author.)

Figure 154. Citadel, Lille, Arsenal, after 1668. (Photo: Author.)

Figure 155. Phalsbourg, Governor's House, ca. 1679. (Photo: Author.)

Figure 156. Citadel, Besançon, Chapel, consecrated 1683. (Photo: Author.)

Figure 157. Citadel, Lille, Powder Magazine, after 1668. (Photo: Author.)

stacked on a paved floor to protect against humidity, small openings assured ventilation while protecting against the entry of projectiles, and nails, hinges, and locks were made of bronze instead of iron to prevent sparks.

Vauban himself was a fascinating figure, a combination of soldier, practical engineer, and free-thinking intellectual. He wrote technical treatises on siege warfare, and among his letters and other voluminous writings can be found specific comments on architecture and fortifications. Some of these are extremely interesting, and reveal Vauban's sensitivity to the symbolic powers of the building arts. In 1681, Louvois complained to him that the designs for the gates of Strasbourg's citadel were "too grand and magnificent," and should be reduced. Vauban, after explaining that the size of the portals could not be altered, and that the criticism could only result in the elimination of decorative details, including the coat-of-arms and monogram of the King, added: "I do not however agree with this advice, seeing that this is the passageway to all of Germany and that the Germans, who are extremely curious and usually good connoisseurs, are the sort of people who judge the King's magnificence and the good quality of the fortress by the beauty of its gates." Yet on a previous occasion, in 1672, he cautioned Louvois not to order a bust of Louis XIV to be set up on the portal of Ath (a recently conquered town) because that would "expose his portrait to injury by the enemy and to the insults of drunkards and the mob"; instead, he suggested that "some other hieroglyph" be used that would be less provocative.

Of great interest to the readers of this book should be Vauban's opinion of the Invalides (Chap. 9). In a *mémoire* of 1691(?) (unpublished during his lifetime), he first praised the institution as exuding greatness and piety, but then found fault with the constrained and austere life that the veterans led there, deprived of "that freedom so much desired, which, in every place and in every time, constitutes more than half of man's happiness and felicity." He continued:

That great courtyard [Fig. 73] where one usually sees 700 to 800 men walking about like people who do not know what to become nor what to do creates a spectacle in the eyes of passersby that has disagreeable associations and an unedifying atmosphere of idleness, which inspires nothing worthy of the nobility of that institution. It is certain that the arrangement of the Invalides, in the state in which it is, does not sufficiently have the desired effect on the spirit of the troops, who consider that establishment as a sort of decent hospital erected for the unfortunates [*les misérables*], where they are only received when they can't go on. That opinion doesn't warm the heart and barely lifts the spirit, because the soldier only sees a very mediocre resource that must cost him his freedom, and the little good that he glimpses there is subject to conditions hard and so dangerous that . . . are . . . undesirable.

As for the *pièce de résistance,* the recently completed Dôme (Figs. 78–9), Vauban's words have the force of a cannon blast: "as for that great and beautiful Dôme that has cost so much, one can only say that it is no more necessary for the Invalides than a fifth wheel on a wagon."

Vauban's comments on the Invalides reveal his intellectual independence and probing mind. These qualities clearly emerge in his views about two pressing issues of his day: the Protestant question and rural poverty. In 1689, he addressed a *mémoire* to Louvois, harshly critical of the Revocation of the Edict of Nantes (1685), which gave French Protestants the choice of either converting to Catholicism or emigrating, and condemned the Revocation on economic, military, and philosophical grounds: "Kings are certainly masters of the lives and welfare of their subjects, but never of their opinions, because private views are beyond their power, and only God can direct them as it pleases Him." As for the poor French peasants whom he observed everywhere on his constant travels throughout the kingdom, Vauban painted their picture in pitiful strokes: "The poorest people rarely drink [wine], don't eat meat three times a year, and [eat] a little salt. . . . It is not surprising that people so badly nourished have so little strength. To which should be added that what they suffer because of nakedness contributes much to this, three-quarters of them dressed in winter and summer only in cloth half-rotten and torn, and clad in wooden shoes so that their feet are exposed all year long."

To alleviate the lot of the poor and solve France's economic problems, Vauban precociously proposed the detailed gathering of regional geographic and economic information, and, in 1706, had printed a book called *Projet d'une dîme royale,* which proposed a uniform tax formula for all French citizens in place of the numerous and complex assortment of exactions from which the privileged could escape and which weighed heavily on the poor. Copies of the book were seized and burned; Vauban, already ill, died the next year. Yet Louis XIV always had had full confidence in his professional powers and had been personally grateful to him for an incident at the front in 1688 when Vauban had prevented the Grand Dauphin from exposing himself to danger in the trenches. When Vauban died, the King lamented, "I have lost a man much loved by my person and by the state." Even that acerbic court gossip, the Duc de Saint-Simon, had only fulsome praise, describing Vauban in 1703 as "perhaps the most honest and most virtuous man of his century and, along with the greatest reputation as the most learned man in the art of sieges and fortification, the simplest, the truest, and the most modest." And Bernard de Fontenelle, of the Royal Academy of Sciences (of which Vauban was an honorary member), in the funeral oration delivered in the church of Saint-Roch in Paris, intoned: "In a word, he was a Roman whom our century, it would seem, had stolen from the happiest days of the Republic."

LE ROI-ARCHITECTE

Given the Monarch's deep involvement with his building projects, it is not surprising that specific works have been attributed to Louis XIV himself. In 1691 one of Hardouin-Mansart's clerks reported that some people claimed that the main ideas for Marly (Chap. 11) were the King's; however, the work was always ascribed by contemporaries to the first architect. Another instance of an attribution to the King was furnished by a garden feature at Versailles, the Bosquet of the Three Fountains (1677–9, destroyed). A contemporary plan bears the anonymous inscription: "de la pensée du Roy, Executé par Monsieur Le Nostre" (the King's idea, executed by Monsieur Le Nostre). Yet, in 1687, the Swedish architect Tessin the Younger, when escorted around the gardens by Le Nôtre himself, was informed by the royal gardener that the design was his; presumably, if the King had had anything to do with it, Le Nôtre would have dutifully reported the fact.

A more intriguing instance is provided by the Colonnade at Versailles (Fig. 92). We know that in April and May 1684, thought was being given to move the sculptures of the soon-to-be-demolished Grotto of Tethys (Fig. 40) to a new garden site for which Mansart offered two projects, one with water basins, another with a columnar pavilion (designs lost). Then, in June, the reliable Marquis de Dangeau reported laconically in his journal: "The King ordered a marble colonnade with big fountains" at this site. The result is the extant structure, which makes no provision for the sculptures, which were placed in another *bosquet*. Did Louis XIV on his own initiative instruct Mansart to abandon the prior suggestions and replace them with an entirely new conception, perhaps only vaguely envisaged? Although contemporary sources assign the work without any qualification to Mansart, we shall return to this possibility later.

A fascinating revelation of how the Sun King actually determined the design of one of his important structures – the Grand or Marble Trianon

(1687; Chap. 10) – has been explicated in an important study (1969) by the French art historian Bertrand Jestaz. The initial idea, which Jestaz attributes to Louis and which is shown in a plan from Mansart's studio (Fig. 99), preserved the pavilions of the Porcelain Trianon (Fig. 56) by linking them together, with oval rooms (suggested by the contour of the original court-yard) connecting the main pavilion (now subdivided into a rectangular room flanked by octagons) to wings formed by joining the lateral pavilions to the small pavilions flanking the initial entrance plaza. Moreover, Jestaz has noted that this plan retained a circulation pattern present at the first Tria-non. To the north of the original Trianon there stood in the garden a vaulted pergola leading to a pavilion, the Perfume Cabinet (Cabinet des Parfums; 1671), where odoriferous flowers were kept. In passing from the Porcelain Trianon into the pergola and then to the Cabinet, the King moved in a

jogged path. This pattern was retained in the first plan for the Marble Trianon and in the final building itself (Figs. 100 and 101) but entirely *within* the structure: from the *corps-de-logis*, the King could enter the barrel-vaulted long gallery (Fig. 108, corresponding to the vaulted pergola, both lit mainly from the *parterre* side), which led at its end to the Salon des Jardins (Salon of Gardens), corresponding in placement (although not in function) to the Cabinet des Parfums. Thus, the first plan was a result of a desire to retain existing structures as well as old habits. Documents uncov-ered by Jestaz prove that Louis XIV – who would seat himself under a tent at the construction site, joined by the Marquis de Louvois (the new superintendent of the King's buildings) – exerted close control over the building and personally intervened so that its design was modified fre-quently. A letter from Louvois to Mansart – written while the building was under construction and the first architect was absent, taking the waters at Vichy (!) – states that the King had ordered the demolition of the central part of the *corps-de-logis* (then six or seven feet high) because he was dissatisfied with its effect when viewed from the garden side. In a drawing from Mansart's office (Fig. 98), this part of the *corps-de-logis* appears at the right. The drawing reveals that the first idea for the elevations included a sequence of rectangular windows surmounted by rectangular bas-reliefs and a visible *mansarde* roof. But in the same letter, Louvois writes that the Monarch had found the roof to be too heavy, giving to Trianon the air of a "grosse maison" (big house); instead, the King wanted roofs that could not be seen, with low chimneys only a foot high. The letter then continues with Louis' critiques of Mansart's drawings that had been sent to him: the entablature of the gallery should match the height of the entablature of the main building (instead of being three feet lower) so that the interior of the gallery will be 24, not 21, feet high; Trianon-sous-Bois (Fig. 101, no. 18 [first version]) should have a low roof like the rest of Trianon. There follow the King's questions concerning the linkage of Trianon-sous-Bois with the Salon des Jardins and the gallery, with Louvois asking Mansart whether the entablature of the gallery should be continued at the same height for the Salon and Trianon-sous-Bois, and whether the edge of the roof should have a socle with pedestals for the placement of "vases or such other ornament that it may please the King to order."

The letter continues with Louvois' own questions about the correspondence of measurements of the gallery elevation with those of the main building. Then the minister reports that "His Majesty would like there to be something very light (*fort léger*), supported by columns in the manner of a peristyle" to replace the central part of the main building that will be demolished. Mansart is to provide drawings at the first opportunity, the King well aware of the fact that Mansart is at the moment taking the waters at Vichy. Louvois adds that the peristyle should serve to close the courtyard and provide a covered link between the two corner rooms (the later Salle des Seigneurs and the Salon Rond or Salon des Colonnes). Louvois concludes the letter by asking Mansart to think about whether the peristyle should be in line with the other buildings on the garden side or whether it should slightly project, and he reminds the first architect to always accommodate his ideas to the solidity of the structure.

This letter was written by Louvois on September 18. Four days later, he dispatched another to Mansart. The latter was informed that because of his absence and the King's eagerness that Trianon be completed, drawings for the peristyle had been requested from Robert de Cotte, Mansart's main assistant and brother-in-law. The drawings were in accord with the King's taste, which demands that the peristyle should not be extremely broad, since its height will be only 24 feet; that its long central axis should align with the *enfilade* of the King's apartment; and that the ends of the peristyle's garden façade should cover a bay of the corner pavilions (containing the Salle des Seigneurs and Salon Rond), so that these pavilions would not appear wider than the Salon des Glaces and the Cabinet du Couchant that frame the entire garden façade (all two bays wide; this subtlety was not executed, but appears in an extant drawing). Louvois continues: De Cotte has presented several drawings to His Majesty, who has selected one of the two that accompany this letter; the second has too many columns. At the same time, the King has ordered construction to begin on the arcaded court elevation of the peristyle. The plan and elevations of the garden façade of the peristyle are included with the letter for Mansart's opinion, and Louvois reminds him that His Majesty strongly wishes to have only columns so that the architecture should be lighter, and that

that part remaining entirely open on the garden side, one might be able from within to enjoy the view of the canal and the entire garden. His Majesty is the more readily disposed to order the beginning of the façade on the court side since the architecture only continues that which you have set and projected for the building that he ordered destroyed, except that you only placed six columns on the court side instead of eight that are shown in this drawing, which appear necessary so that the piers that are behind them correspond to the grouped columns that His Majesty desires on the garden façade.

In a postscript, Louvois reports the arrival of Mansart's reply to the first letter, apparently accompanied by drawings, and Louis XIV's reaction to them. The King is said to be pleased that the first architect's proposal for the peristyle is rather similar to the one ordered by him. The Monarch shall await Mansart's response to the elevations of both sides of the peristyle that will be sent to him. Louvois concludes by pointing out that the entablature of Trianon-sous-Bois must be raised to the same height as the rest of the building in order that the ceiling heights of some of the *chambres* be sufficiently high.

Six days later (September 28), Louvois again wrote to Mansart, now taking the mineral waters at Bourbon, those at Vichy having been of little help. The minister explains that the King has ordered that all three windows of the Salon Rond (and, by necessity, those of the Salle des Seigneurs) will remain exposed on the garden side, but that he does not approve of Mansart's placement of the paired columns on that façade nor of those proposed for the interior of the peristyle, which will considerably narrow it in such a way that it will project only one foot or one and a half feet more than the pavilions, whereas the latter project four feet. In addition, His Majesty does not think it suitable that the peristyle, which is the center of the building, should have single columns, because the pavilions have grouped (i.e., paired) pilasters.

These remarkable letters throw light on Louis XIV's intimate involvement with the Grand Trianon and the early stages of its design, which involved the wholesale destruction of its partially built central section that displeased the Monarch. Most important, it was Louis XIV himself who conceived of a peristyle for this part of the structure, and gave it its name (Figs. 102–5). The King thought of the peristyle as a room entirely open on the garden side, but closed on the court side, corresponding to what we would call a loggia. (It was provided with *portes-fenêtres* until 1701, but these probably were often opened, as a text of 1689 suggests, thus acting like theatrical curtains to reveal the garden beyond [Chap. 10]).

A subsequent letter of Louvois (October 19), addressed to his assistant, Colbert de Villacerf (who was to succeed to Louvois' post in 1691), gives further information about the Sun King's influence on the form of the new Trianon and its garden, details concerning the kind of stone to be used for the balusters and their arrangement; the shapes of rooms; the forms of water basins, the widths of *allées*, the heights of trellises and trees, the placement of fountains; and the shape of the service court, as well as other particulars. In some instances, the King gives his approval to suggestions by his architect and gardener; at other times, he is the inventor of the idea. His thoughts are always communicated verbally or in writing, not by means of drawings.

Returning to Versailles on November 13 from the traditional autumn sojourn at Fontainebleau, Louis changed coaches to ride immediately to Trianon. He found the building to be "very advanced and very beautiful" and was "very content," as reported by the reliable Marquis de Dangeau. The King returned on November 14, 15, 16, and again on November 26, 27, and 29. On December 5, "he walked a good deal in his buildings that he had erected and with which he is very satisfied at this moment." He returned seven more times before the year's end. The new Trianon was virtually complete, although later years saw changes in the interior room arrangements and the remodeling of Trianon-sous-Bois (Fig. 109). In 1701, the *portes-fenêtres* of the court were removed, and the peristyle then served as a permanently open screen integrating the building with its surroundings but at the same time separating it into two semi-independent structures.

The fortunate survival of Louvois' letters has allowed an unusual insight into the genesis and evolution of a royal building of Louis XIV. They also directly reveal the King's personal taste in 1687 for visual and structural lightness of form (no visible roofs; slender columnar supports), and for the importance of providing views (of the garden and canal). Louvois' report that Louis desired a very light (*fort léger*) columnar construction for the center of Trianon brings to mind Mansart's Colonnade for Versailles (Fig. 92), designed three years before, and Dangeau's diary entry that it had been ordered by the King. Is the Colonnade, like the Grand Trianon, also a direct expression of His Majesty's personal taste in the 1680s?

It may be that only at the Grand Trianon did the King truly act as a *roi-architecte*. Future research may lengthen that list, but it is certain that, at the very least, the Sun King's scale of building and his close involvement with all phases of design and construction mark him as one of history's greatest *rois-bâtisseurs* (builder–kings).

ABSOLUTISM AND ARCHITECTURE

The Sun King's lavish building programs found pious justification in the writings of the Bishop of Meaux, Jacques-Bénigne Bossuet, tutor (1670–80) to the King's son, Louis, the Grand Dauphin, and the greatest pulpit orator of his age. In his *Politics Derived from the Words of Holy Scripture* (published posthumously in 1709 but mainly written 1677–9, revised 1700–3), he wrote (in a section on royal riches and finances):

There are expenditures which are necessary, and others which are for splendor and dignity. . . .

One may count, among necessary expenditures, all those required for war, such as fortifications, arsenals, magazines, and munitions, which have been mentioned before.

The expenditures for magnificence and dignity are not less necessary, in their own way, to sustain majesty in the eyes of the people and of foreigners.

It would be an infinite task to recount the magnificence of Solomon.

After a brief paragraph extolling Solomon's temple in Jerusalem, Bossuet turns to the details of the Jewish king's palace there, as recounted in 1(3) Kings 7 and other places in the Old Testament:

Thirteen full years were needed to build the king's palace in Jerusalem, with wood, stone, marbles, and the most precious materials, as well as the most beautiful and richest architecture that was ever seen. It was called the Lebanon because of the great numbers of cedars that were erected there as tall columns like a forest, in vast and long galleries and with a marvelous order.

The royal throne was especially admired, wherein all shone with gold, as in the superb gallery where it was placed. The seat was of ivory covered with the purest gold; the six steps by which one mounted to the throne and the stools for the feet were of the same metal; the ornaments that bordered it were also of solid gold.

Nearby was seen the special place in the gallery where justice was rendered, all built in the same manner.

Solomon at the same time built the palace of the queen, his wife, daughter of Pharaoh, where everything sparkled with precious stones and where one saw an exquisite order gleam with magnificence.

For these beautiful works, this prince summoned from his country as well as from foreign ones the most renowned artisans for design, sculpture, architecture, whose names are consecrated for ever in the records of God's people, that is to say, in holy books.

Let us add the places destined for equipage, where the horses, chariots, carriages were without number.

The tables and the officers of the king's household for hunting, for sustenance, for the entire service, in their number as in their order, corresponded to this magnificence.

The king was served with gold plate. All the vases of the Lebanon were of fine gold. And the Holy Bible does not disdain going into all this detail, because it served, in that time of peace, to make the power of so great a king felt and admired at home and abroad.

. . .

God forbade ostentation inspired by vanity, and the foolish puffing up of a heart drunk with wealth; but he nevertheless wished the courts of kings to shine with magnificence, in order to impress upon the people a certain attitude of respect.

And even today, at the coronation of kings . . . the Church makes this prayer: "May the glorious dignity and the majesty of the palace dazzle the eyes of all beholders with the great splendor of royal power, so that the light shall shine forth on all sides like a star." All these are words chosen to express the magnificence of a royal court which is demanded by God as a necessary support for royalty.

We cannot be certain whether these passages were composed during 1677–9 (when Versailles was beginning to undergo great expansion; Chap. 10) or several decades later. In any event, the palace and court of Solomon as described by Bossuet on the basis of holy writ immediately remind one of Versailles and the Sun King. It is also very interesting to observe that Bossuet translated the Latin word *porticus* (meaning portico and given in the Vulgate) as *galerie*, in describing the room in Solomon's palace where his throne was set up and where justice was dispensed. (In the Galerie des Glaces, a throne was occasionally set up for ambassadorial receptions; cf. Fig. 97.) All French translations available to Bossuet render *porticus* as *portique*, a French word directly derived, of course, from the Latin. Furthermore, Solomon's gold furniture reminds us of the solid silver furniture of Louis (melted down for bullion in 1689 during the War of the League of Augsburg), and Solomon's foreign, Egyptian wife has a counterpart in the Spanish Marie-Thérèse. Most important is that the Bible was used by Bossuet as a means of rationalizing the Sun King's architecture and lavish court.

These passages from Bossuet are significant because he was the prime apologist for the political system of absolute monarchy, the classic embodiment of which is precisely the reign of Louis XIV. In the *Politics,* Bossuet argued that royal authority is sacred, paternal, absolute, and subordinated to reason. The person of the king is sacred and to attack him is sacrilege. He is the representative of divine majesty, the means by which God realizes his purposes on earth. Kingly power, however, must be exercised with fear and self-restraint, for Heaven will demand an ultimate accounting. Royal power is absolute, but absolute government is not arbitrary government. Absolute power allows the ruler to do good and repress evil; innocence will protect individuals from the king's authority. The king is not a private person; he is a public personage, and "all the state is in him; the will of all the people is included in his." The king's power holds the kingdom together; should he withdraw it, the realm would be in confusion. Kings are especially endowed with intelligence so that they may govern with reason. And so Bossuet argues at great length, continually buttressing his points with biblical quotations and references.

In reality, Louis XIV was hemmed in on all sides by law and tradition; he could not simply have his way at all times. Yet, he did succeed, when compared to earlier French kings, in wielding considerable power, particularly over a weakened aristocracy that had challenged royal power during the Fronde, and had lost.

Not all Frenchmen of Louis' time believed, however, that they were living in a golden age or under an ideal system of government. Another priest, Fénelon, severely attacked the King in a famous letter to him, probably written in 1694 (while the War of the League of Augsburg was raging), but probably unread because Louis appointed Fénelon Archbishop of Cambrai the next year. Fénelon accused the King of having impoverished France "in order to introduce to the court a monstrous and incurable luxury." He saw that *gloire* (see Chap. 1) was at the root of the Monarch's disastrous rule:

But, while they [the common people] lack bread, you yourself lack money, and you refuse to see the extreme position to which you are reduced. Since you have always been happy, you cannot imagine that you would ever cease to be so. You are afraid to open your eyes; you are afraid to be compelled to have to diminish some of your *gloire*. That *gloire*, which hardens your heart, is dearer to you than justice, than your own tranquillity, than the survival of your people, who perish daily from sicknesses caused by famine, and finally, than your eternal salvation, which is incompatible with this idol, *gloire*.

*   *   *

The message of monarchical power embodied in the Sun King's creations was very well understood by his contemporaries. The poet Jean de La Fontaine, in magical verses, brings us at sunset to the great terrace at Versailles whence we view the Allée Royale in the presence of the great King and his court (Figs. 42 and 43):

Là, dans des chars dorés, le Prince avec sa cour
Va goûter la fraîcheur sur le déclin du jour.
L'un et l'autre Soleil, unique en son espèce,
Étale aux regardants sa pompe et sa richesse.
Phébus brille à l'envi du monarque françois;
On ne sait bien souvent à qui donner sa voix:
Tous deux sont pleins d'éclat et rayonnants de gloire.
(*The Loves of Psyche and Cupid*, 1669)

(There, in golden chariots, the Prince with his court
Goes to enjoy the freshness at the close of day.
Each sun, unique of his kind,
Spreads over the onlookers his magnificence and splendor.
Phoebus shines in emulation of the French monarch;
Very often one does not know whom to address:
Both are full of pomp and radiant with glory.)

La Fontaine knew how to read royal iconography and symbolism. For him, however, and surely for other Frenchmen, the magnificence of Versailles (and the other royal works) transcended the level of panegyrics to attain a higher plane of aesthetic beauty, the true and lasting accomplishment of the royal arts. The poet, after describing various garden features at Versailles, concludes his verses with an encomium of Le Nôtre's art, and, by extension, of the genius of all Louis XIV's artists:

Heureux ceux de qui l'art a ces traits inventés!
On ne connoissoit point autrefois ces beautés.
Tous parcs étoient vergers du temps de nos ancêtres,
Tous vergers sont faits parcs: le savoir de ces maîtres
Change en jardins royaux ceux des simples bourgeois,
Comme en jardins de dieux il change ceux des rois.
Que ce qu'ils ont planté dure mille ans encore!
Tant qu'on aura des yeux, tant qu'on chérira Flore,
Les nymphes des jardins loueront incessament
Cet art qui les savoit loger si richement.

(Happy are those whose art has invented these forms!
These beauties were not known in past times.
All parks were orchards in our ancestors' times,
All orchards have been made into parks: the skill of these masters
Changes into royal gardens those of simple bourgeois,
As into gardens of the gods it changes those of kings.
May that which they have planted last a thousand years more!
As long as one shall have eyes, so long shall one cherish Flora,
The garden nymphs shall incessantly praise
This art that knows how to house them so richly.)

Yet the achievement of the immense confection that is Versailles exacted an unusually high cost in human life among the workmen. In a famous letter of Madame de Sévigné – the greatest French letter writer of her day – she wrote (October 12, 1678):

The Court is at Saint-Cloud; the King wants to go Saturday to Versailles, but it appears God is not willing, because it is impossible to put the buildings in shape to receive him. This is a result of the prodigious mortality rate among the workmen – cartloads of corpses carried off nightly from Versailles, as from the Charity Hospitals. This grim transport is being concealed in order not to frighten off the work force, in order not to decry the air of that "favorite without merit" [*favori sans mérite*]. You know that *bon mot* about Versailles.

While contemplating Versailles and the other royal buildings and gardens, our moral conscience struggles with our aesthetic perceptions. The hunger of the French peasantry; the corpses of workmen wheeled out of Versailles under cover of darkness; the wasteful wars; the King's overbearing compulsion for *gloire* – these and other thoughts stir within us, tarnishing the luster of France's golden age. Yet the great enterprises remain to move and give delight to all who have eyes. Surely Mansart, Le Nôtre, the other royal artists, and yes, great Louis himself, all knew that long after the Sun King's deeds were but dimly remembered or even forgotten, his name would survive the ages through the power of art.

EPILOGUE
The Old King in Triumph and Sorrow

On Saturday, August 28, 1706, an inaugural Mass was celebrated in the Dôme of the Invalides. The auspicious occasion was marked by a visit of the King (then sixty-eight years old) and members of his family and court. As the royal entourage approached the church, the scene must have closely resembled an earlier royal visit to the Invalides of 1701 (recorded in a painting, Fig. 158). Six hundred veterans, residents of the Hôtel of the Invalides, dressed in their uniforms and bearing arms, lined the approach. Drums and trumpets sounded as the royal coaches drew near. Louis XIV descended at the foot of the outdoor stair to see, assembled on the top landing, the architect Hardouin-Mansart, officers from the royal building administration, and other royal architects, sculptors, and painters who had collaborated in the great work. In an unusual gesture, Mansart presented an ornate gold key to His Majesty and delivered a short speech (duly recorded, as well as the entire ceremony, in the *Mercure galant*):

I have the honor to present at the feet of Your Majesty the key to this sacred temple, which Your piety has erected to the glory of God. I shall be happy if this work that you have consigned to my care for thirty years can respond to the high idea that Your Majesty gave to me and to his wise advice. This superb monument to your religion shall indicate to the most distant posterity the greatness of your reign.

The King listened attentively and then returned the key to the architect as an expression of his satisfaction. His Majesty then entered the Dôme, received holy water from the archbishop, and then noticed Mansart's wife and family amid the throng within. He approached her and said:

Madame, seeing you here, I cannot refrain from complimenting you for the share that you must take in the glory that Monsieur your husband is receiving today.

Figure 158. Pierre-Denis Martin, *Visit of Louis XIV to the Invalides, 1701,* 1701.
Musée Carnavalet, Paris. (Photo: Photothèque des Musées de la Ville de Paris.)

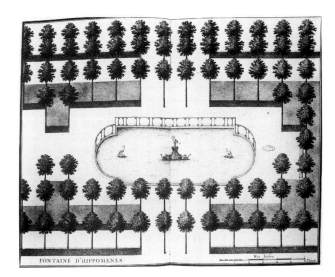

Figure 159. Hippomenes Fountain, Marly, from 1702 and later. Drawing, Archives Nationales, Paris. (Photo: from *Monuments Historiques,* 1982.)

We are told that the King then inspected the completed interior and was "struck with astonishment." A *Te Deum* and Mass (with music by Michel-Richard Delalande) followed, the musicians lodged on balconies above the curved entablatures of the crossing piers (Fig. 79). Upon leaving the building, Louis spent a quarter hour admiring the façade (Fig. 78) despite the rain, gave Mansart "a thousand marks of his benevolence and satisfaction," and mounted into his carriage. As he rode off, the King must have been aglow with contentment at the completion of one of the major projects of his reign (Chap. 9).

Two years later, in 1708, Mansart died at Marly. The ceremony at the Invalides was to be the last of its kind for Louis, who was on the verge of a horrendous series of personal losses as devastating as anything found in Greek tragedy. Between 1711 and 1714, disease (smallpox and measles) and other afflictions struck down his son, the Grand Dauphin, two of his grandsons (the Ducs de Bourgogne and de Berry, sons of the Grand Dauphin), the adored wife of the Duc de Bourgogne, the Duchesse de Bourgogne (Marie-Adélaïde de Savoie), and two great-grandsons, one at five years, the other at twenty days. The succession, which everyone had expected to pass to the Grand Dauphin (who was fifty in 1711), devolved in 1715 upon the head of a child of five, Louis XIV's great-grandson Louis, duc d'Anjou, the second son of the Duc de Bourgogne, who became Louis XV.

During these terrible years, the King ordered masses and public prayers throughout the kingdom, closed theaters, ended spectacles, and opened up his grieving heart to a trusted official, the Duc de Villars, who recorded Louis as saying, "I have merited it [the losses], and I will suffer less in the next world."

Figure 160. Nicolas Coustou, *Boar Hunter*, Marly, Park. (Photo: Author.)

During this dark time, Louis XIV had no great architectural enterprises to which to attend; instead, he continued to busy himself with adjustments and revisions of the garden of Marly (Chap. 11). The Duc d'Antin (a bastard son by Madame de Montespan), who succeeded Mansart as superintendent in 1708, wrote in 1727:

There were at Marly two types of fountains. The first adorned the most beautiful garden ever made for its size, the others had been made in order to occupy the late King during his hours of relaxation [*délassement*], not having any other amusement.

The second type of fountain alluded to here surely includes the carp-ponds, created in 1702 between the King's Pavilion and the great cascade. These four elongated water basins (Fig. 159) were stocked with carp, incredibly long-lived fish with royal associations. The carp-ponds underwent continuous changes during the remainder of the Sun King's reign. Central islands were inserted in them, eventually adorned with running figures from mythology (Hippomenes and Atalanta, Apollo and Daphne), with alterations made again and again to their bases and other details. The celebrated diarist of the reign, the Duc de Saint-Simon, wrote in 1715 that "Goldfish [carp] ponds, decorated with gilding and delightful paintings, were scarcely finished before they were unmade and rebuilt differently by the same artists, and such things were done over and over again." (By "paintings," Saint-Simon surely meant the colored glazed tiles used to revet the basins.)

The continual tinkering with these ponds can only have proceeded at the King's command, and we may surmise that these garden features not only gave him pleasure, but also provided an outlet for his creative impulses.

That Louis sometimes took an active role in formulating thoughts for Marly is attested by a letter (1706?) by the sculptor Nicolas Coustou, who wrote about his "two groups of hunters, the ideas for which were given by His Majesty himself, that I have tried to follow exactly . . ." (one of these groups is shown in Fig. 160). At the carp-ponds and at other locations in the garden, minor changes proceeded. The great architectural undertakings were in the past. At the end of his long reign, the grieving King tended his favorite garden like a mourner embellishing the tomb of a beloved.

GLOSSARY

English-language architectural terms not found here can be found in any standard architectural dictionary.

Allée: A garden avenue.

Architectonic: Relating to the purely architectural or structural features of a design, as opposed to the decorative or nonstructural.

Avant-corps: A projecting block or pavilion.

Bienséance: Architectural decorum, or the suitability of a form to its function (virtually synonymous with *convenance*).

Bosquet: An enclosed and wooded garden precinct.

Colossal order: An order that extends through more than one story (see *Order*).

Convenance: See *Bienséance*.

Corps-de-logis: The main living unit of a house or château.

Deuxième étage: The second floor in English usage, the third floor in American.

Drum: A vertical wall supporting a dome or vault. It is usually circular in plan, but may be square or polygonal.

Enfilade: A linear suite or vista within a building, the latter created by a sequence of doors in alignment.

Faubourg: A suburb immediately outside the city walls.

Hôtel: A substantial town house or mansion.

Maison de plaisance: A house meant for recreational living.

Mansarde roof: A visible roof of double slope, the lower longer and steeper than the upper. Rooms can be accommodated under the roof.

Order: In classical architecture, a column or pilaster with base (usually), shaft, capital, and entablature, proportioned and detailed according to a mode (Doric, Tuscan, Ionic, Corinthian, Composite).

Parterre: A garden bed.

Parterre d'eau: A garden bed in the form of a pool of water.

Parterre de broderie: A garden bed composed of shrubs in elaborate patterns.

Place: An urban square.

Place royale: An urban square dedicated to the king, usually with a central monument in his honor.

Porte-fenêtre: A French window.

Premier étage: The first floor in English usage, the second floor in American.

Retrochoir: The space behind the high altar in a large church.

Rustication: Masonry in the form of massive, rough blocks.

Spandrel: The quasi-triangular space between the outer curve of an arch and its rectangular frame, or the space between two adjacent arches and the horizontal molding above.

Vermiculated: Masonry decorated with irregular shallow grooves like worm tracks.

BIBLIOGRAPHICAL GUIDE

For the history of French architecture in general during the Louis XIV era, see L. Hautecoeur, *Histoire de l'architecture classique en France. II: Le règne de Louis XIV,* 2 vols., Paris, 1948, and the relevant sections in A. Blunt, *Art and Architecture in France, 1500 to 1700,* 4th ed., Harmondsworth, 1980, and in J.-M. Pérouse de Montclos, *Histoire de l'architecture française. De la Renaissance à la Révolution,* Paris, 1989. The history of French gardens of this period is surveyed in W. H. Adams, *The French Garden, 1500–1800,* New York, 1979, and in K. Woodbridge, *Princely Gardens: The Origins and Development of the French Formal Style,* New York, 1986. Much detailed information about the royal gardens and especially about their hydraulic features can be found in G. Weber, *Brunnen und Wasserkünste in Frankreich im Zeitalter von Louis XIV,* Worms, 1985. For developments in urbanism, see the bibliography for Chapter 7.

During the personal rule of Louis XIV (1661–1715), there were effectively only two first architects of the King: Louis Le Vau (1612–70) and Jules Hardouin-Mansart (1646–1708). There is no comprehensive monograph on Le Vau and only one (unsatisfactory) on Mansart (P. Bourget and G. Cattaui, *Jules Hardouin Mansart,* Paris, 1960). However, there is a substantial section devoted to him in the publication by Hautecoeur cited before, II, 527–688. On the royal garden designer André Le Nôtre (1613–1700), see F. H. Hazlehurst, *Gardens of Illusion. The Genius of André Le Nostre,* Nashville, 1980. Recent short articles on these artists and others mentioned in the text may be found in A. K. Placzek, ed., *Macmillan Encyclopedia of Architects,* 4 vols., New York and London, 1982. Much material on the royal projects of the Sun King appears in A. Laprade, *François d'Orbay, architecte de Louis XIV,* Paris, 1960, but the author's extravagant claims for d'Orbay as the real designer of most of the royal buildings must be discounted; unfortunately, the book lacks an index.

Material on virtually all the topics discussed in the present book will be found in the titles just listed.

CHAPTER 2

LOUIS XIV'S EDUCATION

H. Carré, *The Early Life of Louis XIV (1638–1661),* trans. D. Bolton, London, 1951.

J. B. Wolf, "The Formation of a King," in J. C. Rule, ed., *Louis XIV and the Craft of Kingship,* pp. 102–31, Columbus, Ohio, 1969.

MAZARIN AND THE ARTS

M. Laurain-Portemer, *Études Mazarines,* Paris, 1981.

COURT BALLETS

R. Astier, "Louis XIV, 'Premier Danseur,' " in D. L. Rubin, ed., *Sun King: The Ascendancy of French Culture During the Reign of Louis XIV*, pp. 73–102, Washington, D.C., 1992.

C. I. Silin, *Benserade and His "Ballets de Cour,"* Baltimore, 1940.

ICONOGRAPHY OF THE SUN KING

P. Burke, *The Fabrication of Louis XIV*, New Haven and London, 1992.

L. Hautecoeur, *Louis XIV roi-soleil*, Paris, 1953.

A. Joly, "Le roi-soleil: Histoire d'une image," *Revue de l'histoire de Versailles et de Seine-et-Oise*, 38 (1936): 213–35.

E. Kantorowicz, "Oriens Augusti – Lever du Roi," *Dumbarton Oaks Papers*, 17 (1963): 119–77.

I. Lavin, "Bernini's Image of the Sun King," in *Past – Present: Essays on Historicism in Art from Donatello to Picasso*, pp. 139–200, Berkeley, Los Angeles, and Oxford, 1993.

A.-M. Lecoq, "La symbolique de l'état. Les images de la monarchie des premiers Valois à Louis XIV," in P. Nora, ed., *Les lieux de mémoire. II La nation*, pp. 145–92, esp. pp. 177f., Paris, 1986.

J.-P. Néraudau, *L'Olympe du roi-soleil. Mythologie et idéologie royale au Grand Siècle*, Paris, 1986.

CHAPTER 3

Louis XIV, *Mémoires for the Instruction of the Dauphin*, trans. and ed. P. Sonnino, New York and London, 1970 (for the years 1661–8).

VAUX-LE-VICOMTE

J. Cordey, *Vaux-le-Vicomte*, Paris, 1924.

COLBERT

[Paris, Ministère de la culture], *Colbert 1619–1683*, exhibition catalog, Paris, 1983.

ROYAL BUILDING ADMINISTRATION

R. Guillemet, *Essai sur la surintendance des bâtiments du roi sous le règne personnel de Louis XIV (1662–1715)*, dissertation, University of Paris, Paris, 1912.

PETITE ACADEMIE

R. W. Berger, *In the Garden of the Sun King. Studies on the Park of Versailles under Louis XIV*, chap. 2, Washington, D.C., 1985.

J. Jacquiot, *Médailles et jetons de Louis XIV, d'après le manuscrit de Londres add. 31.908*, 1, pp. i–xxii, Paris, 1968.

ROYAL ACADEMY OF ARCHITECTURE

F. Blondel, *Cours d'architecture enseigné dans l'Académie royale d'architecture*, 5 parts, Paris, 1675–83 (facsimile ed. 1982).

H. Lemonnier, ed., *Procès-verbaux de l'Académie royale d'architecture*, 10 vols., Paris, 1911–29.

H. Millon, "The French Academy of Architecture: Foundation and Program," in J. Hargrove, ed., *French Academy, Classicism and its Antagonists*, pp. 68–77, Newark, Del., 1990.

CHAPTER 4

R. W. Berger, *The Palace of the Sun: The Louvre of Louis XIV*, University Park, Pa., 1993.

D. del Pesco, *Il Louvre di Bernini nella Francia di Luigi XIV*, Naples, 1984.

L. Hautecoeur, *Le Louvre et les Tuileries de Louis XIV*, Paris and Brussels, 1927. *Histoire du Louvre. Le château – Le palais – Le musée des origines à nos jours, 1200–1928*, Paris, [1928].

I. Lavin, "Bernini's Image of the Sun King," in *Past – Present: Essays on Historicism in Art from Donatello to Picasso*, pp. 139–200, Berkeley, Los Angeles, and Oxford, 1993.

N. Sainte Fare Garnot, *Le décor des Tuileries sous le règne de Louis XIV*, Paris, 1988.

CHAPTER 5

M. C. Donnelly, *A Short History of Astronomical Observatories*, Eugene, Oregon, 1973.

R. Hahn, *The Anatomy of a Scientific Institution. The Paris Academy of Sciences, 1666–1803*, Berkeley, Los Angeles, London, 1971.

M. Petzet, "Claude Perrault als Architekt des Pariser Observatoriums," *Zeitschrift für Kunstgeschichte*, 30 (1967): 1–54.

C. Wolf, *Histoire de l'Observatoire de Paris de sa fondation à 1793*, Paris, 1902.

CHAPTER 6

R. W. Berger, *Versailles: The Château of Louis XIV*, University Park, Pa., and London, 1985.
  In the Garden of the Sun King: Studies on the Park of Versailles Under Louis XIV, Washington D.C., 1985.
Y. Bottineau, *Versailles, miroir des princes*, Paris, 1989.
P. de Nolhac, *La création de Versailles*, Versailles, 1901.
  Histoire du château de Versailles. Versailles sous Louis XIV, 2 vols. Paris, 1911.
  Histoire du château de Versailles, 2 vols., Paris, 1925.
F. Gébelin, *Versailles*, Paris, 1964.
A. Marie, *Naissance de Versailles. Le château. Les jardins*, 2 vols., Paris, 1968.
A. Marie and J. Marie, *Mansart à Versailles*, 2 vols., Paris, 1972.
  Versailles au temps de Louis XIV, Paris, 1976.
J.-M. Pérouse de Montclos, *Versailles*, Paris, 1991. (English ed. New York, 1991).
P. Verlet, *Versailles*, Paris, 1961.
G. Walton, *Louis XIV's Versailles*, Chicago, 1986.

CHAPTERS 7 and 12

GENERAL

L. Bernard, *The Emerging City. Paris in the Age of Louis XIV*, Durham, N.C., 1970.
R. Chartier et al., *La ville classique de la renaissance aux révolutions*, Histoire de la France urbaine, Vol. 3, Paris, 1981.
G. Dethan, *Paris sous Louis XIV*, Nouvelle histoire de Paris, Paris, 1990.
E. A. Gutkind, *Urban Development in Western Europe: France and Belgium*, International History of City Development, Vol. 5, New York and London, 1970.
P. Lavedan, *Histoire de l'urbanisme à Paris*, Nouvelle histoire de Paris, Paris, 1975.
P. Lavedan et al., *L'urbanisme à l'époque moderne, XVIe – XVIIIe siècles*, Bibliothèque de la Société française d'archéologie, Vol. 13, Paris, 1982.

O. Ranum, *Paris in the Age of Absolutism*, New York, 1968.

Many of these titles contain background material for Paris during the Louis XIV period; to these should be added D. Thomson, *Renaissance Paris*, Berkeley and Los Angeles, 1984, and H. Ballon, *The Paris of Henri IV*, Cambridge, Mass., and London, 1991.

SPECIFIC FEATURES

A. M. de Boislisle, "Notices historiques sur la Place des Victoires et sur la Place de Vendôme," *Mémoires de la Société de l'histoire de Paris et de l'Ile-de-France*, 15 (1888): 1–272.
G. Despierres, "Construction du Pont-Royal de Paris (1685–1688)," *Mémoires de la Société de l'histoire de Paris et de l'Ile-de-France*, 22 (1895): 179–224.
R. Josephson, "Les projets pour la place Vendôme," *L'Architecture*, 41, no. 3 (1928): 83–91.
K. M. Kantorska, "La Bibliothèque du Roi place Vendôme, du projet à l'échec," *Revue de la Bibliothèque Nationale*, 34 (Winter 1989): 51–5.
M. Petzet, "Das Triumphbogenmonument für Ludwig XIV. auf der Place du Trône," *Zeitschrift für Kunstgeschichte*, 45 (1982): 145–94.

CHAPTER 8

R. W. Berger, *Antoine Le Pautre: A French Architect of the Era of Louis XIV*, Chap. 10, New York, 1969.
P. Bonnassieux, *Le château de Clagny et Madame de Montespan . . .*, Paris, 1881.
C. Harlay, *Le château de Clagny à Versailles*, Versailles, [1912].
A. Marie and J. Marie, *Mansart à Versailles*, I, Chap. I, Paris, 1972.
P. de Nolhac, "Clagny," *Revue de l'histoire de Versailles et de Seine-et-Oise*, 2 (1900): 81–93. (Reprinted in his *La création de Versailles*, pp. 193–7, Versailles, 1901.)
[G. Walton et al.], *Versailles à Stockholm*, Exhibition Catalog, pp. 107–14, Stockholm, 1985.

CHAPTER 9

A. J. Braham, "L'Eglise du Dome," *Journal of the Warburg and Courtauld Institutes*, 23 (1960): 216–24.

L. Dimier, *L'Hôtel des Invalides*, 2d ed., Paris, [1928].

L. Hautecoeur, "L'origine du Dôme des Invalides," *L'Architecture*, 37 (1924): 353–60.

M. Holst, "Zur Ideen- und Baugeschichte des Dôme des Invalides in Paris," *Architectura*, 13 (1983): 41–56.

B. Jestaz, "Jules Hardouin-Mansart et l'église des Invalides," *Gazette des beaux-arts*, ser. 6, 66 (1965): 59–74.

L'Hôtel et l'église des Invalides, Paris, 1990.

P. Reuterswärd, *The Two Churches of the Hôtel des Invalides*, Stockholm, 1965.

R. Strandberg, "Libéral Bruand et les problèmes que soulèvent l'Eglise des Soldats et le Dôme des Invalides," *Konsthistorisk Tidskrift*, 35 (1966): 1–22.

CHAPTER 10

Louis XIV, *Manière de montrer les jardins de Versailles*, ed. S. Hoog, Paris, 1982. (See the review of this edition by R. W. Berger in *Journal of Garden History*, 4 [1984]: 429–31.)

GALERIE DES GLACES

R. W. Berger, *Versailles: The Château of Louis XIV*, Chap. VI, University Park, Pa., and London, 1985.

S. Damiron, "Les dessins originaux de groupes d'un tableau de Lebrun 'Le Roi gouverne par lui-même' de la Galerie de Versailles," in *Études et documents sur l'art français du XIIe au XIXe siècle*, pp. 87–90 Paris, 1959, (*Archives de l'art français*, n.s., 22 [1950–7]).

P. de Nolhac, "L'art de Versailles. La Galerie des Glaces," *La revue de l'art ancien et moderne*, 13 (1903): 177–91, 279–90.

F. Kimball, "Mansart and Le Brun in the Genesis of the Grande Galerie de Versailles," *Art Bulletin*, 22 (1940): 1–6.

J. Langner, "Die Deckenbilder der Spiegelgalerie im Schloss von Versailles," *Kunstgeschichtliche Gesellschaft zu Berlin: Sitzungsberichte*, n.s. 19 (1970/1): 9–11.

"Le Brun interprète de l'histoire de Louis XIV: A propos d'un tableau de la Galerie des Glaces à Versailles," *Formes* (Spring 1982): 21–6.

A. Leclerc, "Charles Le Brun (1619–1690). Son oeuvre et son influence sur les arts au XVIIe siècle," *Versailles illustrée*, 8 (April 1903–March 1904): 99–105.

P. Moisy, "Note sur la Galerie des Glaces," *XVIIe siècle*, no. 53 (1961): 42–50.

W. Vitzthum, *Charles Le Brun e la sua scuola a Versailles*, Milan and Geneva, 1965.

TRIANON DE MARBRE (GRAND TRIANON)

P. de Nolhac, *Les grands palais de France. Les Trianons*, Paris, [1913].

L. Deshairs, *Le Grand Trianon*, Paris, [1908].

B. Jestaz, "Le Trianon de Marbre ou Louis XIV architecte," *Gazette des beaux-arts*, ser. 6, 74 (1969): 259–86.

R. Josephson, "Le Grand Trianon d'après des documents inédits," *Revue de l'histoire de Versailles et de Seine-et-Oise*, 29 (1927): 5–23.

F. Kimball, "La transformation des appartements de Trianon sous Louis XIV," *Gazette des beaux-arts*, ser. 6, 19 (1938): 87–110.

M. Magnien, "Le Trianon de Marbre pendant le règne de Louis XIV," *Revue de l'histoire de Versailles et de Seine-et-Oise*, 10 (1908): 1–30.

A. Marie and J. Marie, *Versailles au temps de Louis XIV*, Chaps. I–IX, Paris, 1976.

D. Meyer, "A propos du péristyle du Grand Trianon," *Revue de l'art*, no. 15 (1972): 79–80.

A. Schnapper, *Tableaux pour le Trianon de Marbre*, Paris, 1967.

[G. Walton et al.], *Versailles à Stockholm*, Exhibition Catalog, pp. 115–26, Stockholm, 1985.

CHAPEL

P. de Nolhac, *La chapelle royale de Versailles*, 2 vols., Versailles and Paris, [1912].

L. Deshairs, "Documents inédits sur la chapelle du château de Versailles (1689–1772)," *Revue de l'histoire de Versailles et de Seine-et-Oise*, 7 (1905): 241–62; 8 (1906): 61–85.

F. Kimball, "The Chapels of the Château of Versailles," *Gazette des beaux-arts*, ser. 6, 26 (1944): 315–32.

A. Marie and J. Marie, *Versailles au temps de Louis XIV*, Chap. XXIII, Paris, 1976.

M. Petzet, "Quelques projets inédits pour la chapelle de Versailles," *Art de France*, 1 (1961): 315–19.

P. Pradel, "Le symbolisme de la chapelle de Versailles," *Bulletin monumental*, 96 (1937): 335–55.

[G. Walton et al.], *Versailles à Stockholm*, Exhibition Catalog, pp. 81–98, Stockholm, 1985.

On interior decoration and the birth of the Rococo, see F. Kimball, *The Creation of the Rococo*, Philadelphia, 1943, and B. Pons, *De Paris à Versailles 1699–1736. Les sculpteurs ornemanistes parisiens et l'art décoratif des Bâtiments du roi*, Strasbourg, 1986.

CHAPTER 11

R. Josephson, "Le plan primitif de Marly," *Revue de l'histoire de Versailles et de Seine-et-Oise*, 30 (1928): 27–46.

J. Marie and A. Marie, *Marly*, Paris, 1947.

C. Mauricheau-Beaupré, "Le Château de Marly," *Gazette illustrée des amateurs des jardins* (1926–7): 1–15.

B. Rosasco, "The Sculptures of Marly and the Programme of Versailles: Considerations of Their Relationship and Meaning," *Journal of Garden History*, 3 (1983): 301–16.

"The Sculptural Decorations of the Garden of Marly: 1679–1699," *Journal of Garden History*, 4 (1984): 95–125.

The Sculptures of the Château of Marly During the Reign of Louis XIV, New York and London, 1986.

G. Weber, "Der Garten von Marly (1679–1715)," *Wiener Jahrbuch für Kunstgeschichte*, 28 (1975): 55–105.

"Le domaine de Marly," *Monuments historiques de la France*, no. 122 (August–September 1982): 81–96.

Brunnen und Wasserkünste in Frankreich im Zeitalter von Louis XIV, pp. 226–240 and passim, Worms, 1985.

CHAPTER 13

L. Grodecki, "Vauban, urbaniste," *XVIIᵉ siècle*, nos. 36–7 (1957): 329–52.

P. Lazard, *Vauban, 1633–1707*, Paris, 1934.

M. Parent, *Vauban, un encyclopédiste avant la lettre*, Paris, 1982.

V. Scully, *Architecture: The Natural and the Manmade*, Chap. 10, New York, 1991.

For technical background on siege warfare, see C. Duffy, *Fire and Stone: The Science of Fortress Warfare 1660–1860*, London and Vancouver, 1975; C. Duffy, *The Fortress in the age of Vauban and Frederick the Great, 1660–1789*, Boston, 1985; and N. Faucherre, *Places fortes, bastion du pouvoir*, 3d ed., Paris, 1990. On the *plans-reliefs*, see C. Brisac, *Le musée des plans – reliefs, Hôtel national des Invalides*, Paris, 1981, and A. de Roux et al., *Les plans en relief des places du roy*, Paris, 1989.

CHAPTER 14

J. Autin, *Louis XIV architecte*, Paris, 1981.

B. Jestaz, "Le Trianon de Marbre ou Louis XIV architecte," *Gazette des beaux-arts*, ser. 6, 74 (1969): 259–86.

INDEX

Note: Page numbers in bold italics refer to illustrations.

Index

Index